The Sculpey Way

with Polymer Clay

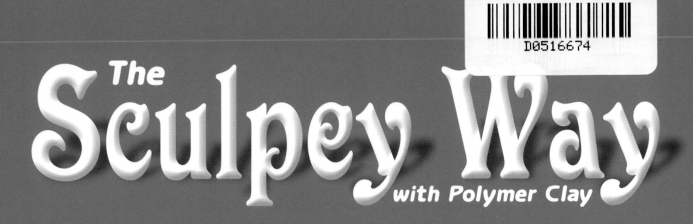

While polymer clay comes in plain little blocks, you'll be amazed at the cute, colorful, charming and clever projects you can make from them! To keep the process even easier, here are step-by-step photos matching the instructions. It's all right here just for you!

Polymer clay is a man-made material, which is great for sculpting because it can be baked in your own oven instead of a kiln.

The pieces in this book are made with clays from the Sculpey® line of polymer clay. the many colors available allow you to create anything— either straight from the package or mixed with other colors to achieve just the right shade. Because each type of clay (Sculpey III, Granitex and Premo!) has slightly different baking directions, please read the packaging for optimum results.

We're proud to offer you this Sculpey® collection by six designers. We hope you'll have a great time making these projects and exploring this Sculpey® world!

The publisher and designers would like to thank the following companies for providing materials used in this publication:
▶ **Artistic Wire Ltd.®** for wire
▶ **Clearsnap Inc.** for ColorBox® pigment ink
▶ **Craf-t Products** for metallic rub ons
▶ **DecoArt™** for opalescent Glamour Glitter Dust
▶ **Duncan Enterprises, Inc.** for Aleene's Original Tacky Glue
▶ **Eclectic Products, Inc.** for E6000®
▶ **Halcraft USA** for beads
▶ **Hero Arts** for rubber stamps
▶ **Inkadinkado** for rubber stamps
▶ **Kemper Tools®, Inc.** for clay cutters
▶ **Marvy® Uchida** for snowflake punch
▶ **McGill, Inc.** for holly leaf punch
▶ **Plaid Enterprises** for the flocking kit, paints
▶ **Polyform Products, Co., Inc.** for Sculpey®, Super Sculpey™, Sculpey III®, Granitex, Premo! Sculpey®
▶ **S. Axelrod Company** for charms
▶ **Slomon's** for SOBO craft glue
▶ **Westrim® Crafts** for wire
▶ **Westwater® Ent.** for rubber stamp

PRODUCTION CREDITS:
▶ **President:** Paulette Jarvey
▶ **Vice-president:** Teresa Nelson
▶ **Production Manager:** Lynda Hill
▶ **Project editors:** Lee Shaw, India Mayo
▶ **Technical editors:** LeNae Gerig, Mary Marget Hite, Susan Cobb
▶ **Photographer:** John McNally
▶ **Graphic designer:** Jacie Pete
▶ **Digital imager:** Victoria Weber

published by:

HOT OFF THE PRESS INC.

Hot Off The Press wants to be kind to the environment. Whenever possible we follow the 3 R's—reduce, reuse and recycle. We use soy and UV inks that greatly reduce the release of volatile organic solvents.

For a color catalog of over 800 products, send $2.00 to:

HOT OFF THE PRESS INC.
1250 N.W. Third, Dept. B
Canby, Oregon 97013
phone (800) 227-9595
fax (503) 266-8749
www.craftpizazz.com

ABOUT THE DESIGNERS:

Anita Behnen discovered polymer clay about 12 years ago. In 1993 she started her clay business, A. Bean Production, and now sells her creations at arts and crafts shows in Dayton, Ohio where she lives with her husband Michael and a menagerie of pets. In addition, Anita designs for craft companies.

Shelly Comiskey lives in a small Chicago suburb with her husband Mike and two children, Casey and Mickey. Through her business, "Simply Shelly," she sells her clay characters in local craft stores. In addition, Shelly designs for craft companies and has appeared in a video.

Shohreh Dolkhani was raised in Pocatello, Idaho but recently made her home in California. She is a registered nurse, but admits that her work simply supports her craft habits. She has two "babies": a chow chow named Daisy and a cocker spaniel named Jamie. Shohreh has been designing clay figures for about five years and has had great success selling her figures and other crafts.

Judy Ferrill has worked with bread dough for years, while raising her three sons, Michael, Casey and Jason. She has taught classes and created pieces for trade shows and product development. She has worked on community bazaars and state fairs.

Sara Naumann lives in Portland, Oregon with her husband Keith and their cat, Bean. She is addicted to rubber stamps and loves to find new ways to use them (like with polymer clay!). She is the Marketing Director at Hot Off The Press, and feels lucky to be surrounded by creative people every day when she comes to work.

Linda Welsh lives in a suburb of Springfield, MO with her two children Alex and Mariah. She began sculpting dolls as a stress reliever when Mariah was in the hospital receiving chemotherapy treatments. To date, Mariah's health is great and she remains in remission. Mariah also enjoys working alongside her mother making figures of her own.

Hot Off The Press and the designers would like to dedicate this book to the memory of Chuck Steinmann, President and Owner of Polyform Products, creators of Sculpey® Polymer Clay.

3

Table of Contents

GENERAL DIRECTIONS: Please read first!

Work surface: A laminated plastic (Formica®) table or counter is ideal. Glass, marble or smooth wood will also work—Sculpey® may damage the finish on some wood surfaces. Use masking tape to attach a sheet of waxed paper or oven parchment for an easily replaced work surface. Be aware that a cold work surface will stiffen the clay.

Cleanliness: Keep your work area clean; it helps to have pre-moistened towelettes available to clean your hands and wipe surfaces between colors. Take special care with white, reds and black. Keep your clay and kitchen equipment separate—once a tool has been used for Sculpey® it should not be used for food preparation. Do not eat while working with clay (this keeps crumbs out of your clay and clay out of you).

Measuring: In this book clay is measured in balls and logs. A 1" ball is one inch through the center. A 1/4" log is 1/4" thick and whatever length you find convenient to handle. A 1/4"x3" log is 1/4" thick and 3" long. The quickest way to make small balls of a given size is to cut them 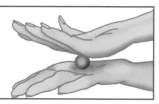 from a log. If you need 1/4" balls, roll a 1/4" log and cut slices just a hair under 1/4" long, then roll into balls.

Warm it first! Warmth is the key to changing firm blocks of Sculpey® into a workable putty-like substance. Warm it in your hands, in a pocket, or sit on it while you're reading these instructions! To hurry it along, place small chunks in a plastic bag in warm water. Be careful—anything that feels hot to the touch may begin to cure Sculpey®. Microwave ovens are not recommended.

Condition it: Sculpey® must be softened and kneaded to make it pliable and not crumbly. Cut the clay into small pieces. Knead one piece until soft, then add the next and continue. A food processor can be very useful to speed up the conditioning process. Process only one package at a time. When the clay forms little balls, like cottage cheese, put it on your work surface and knead it thoroughly.

Blending: Roll softened clay into logs. Lay logs of different colors side by side. Twist them, fold them in half and roll them smooth again. Eventually, the colors will blend into a new shade. If you can't find a shade used in this book, blend the color using this method.

Flattening: Use your fingers to flatten the clay into a rough rectangle of the needed width. Stack craft sticks in the thickness you desire on the sides of the clay. Then use a rolling tool or the smooth handle of an X-acto® knife to flatten the clay between sheets of wax paper to an even 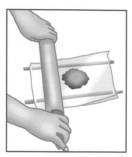 thickness. You can use a pasta machine for smooth, uniformly flat pieces. The #2 setting is about 1/8" thick and the #4 is about 1/16".

Using patterns: You can: (1) Tape waxed paper or oven parchment over the page and shape the clay on it. (2) Trace the pattern onto paper, cut it out, lay the paper on a sheet of clay and cut around it.

Baking: Follow the manufacturer's directions for time and oven temperature. Bake in a glass or ceramic baking dish or on an insulated or doubled cookie sheet. Place cooking parchment under the pieces to prevent shiny spots, and to prevent the clay from touching surfaces which may later be used for food. Leave at least 1" between projects.

Adding Support: Many of the projects in this book need a little extra support or they will fall over while baking. The easiest way to add support is to insert a toothpick into the center of one piece and place the next piece on it. It is also a good idea to support the piece while it is baking. Use a pre-baked piece of clay, more toothpicks or crumpled aluminum foil as support.

To check: You can't tell if Sculpey® is done until it has cooled completely. Bake a test piece of scrap clay with your sculptures. Try to bend it—does it break easily? Underbaked Sculpey® is fragile, like pie crust. Re-bake if your test piece seems underdone.

GENERAL TECHNIQUES

Antique: Mix one part water to one part dark brown acrylic paint. Working quickly, paint the project with the wash being careful not to paint hair or bows. Wipe the project with a soft cloth to remove the wash from surfaces but leaving it to dry in cracks. If the wash dries too quickly, re-wet with water.

Attaching Pieces: Follow the project instructions to shape each piece. Use a ½"-1" toothpick length to join and reinforce the head and body.

Chalking: Use chalk to blush cheeks and raised areas. Soft pastel chalks work best; they're often sold in sets. Rub a small soft paintbrush on the chalk, then lightly stroke it onto the unbaked clay. "Shading" is chalking a darker color in creases, around the eyes and at the mouth.

Collar Bow: Form fabric strip into a circle, crossing the ends at the bottom. Pinch together to form a bow and adjust the loop sizes and tail lengths. Tie the center with a wire length twisted to secure it in back.

Bead Eyes: Inserting seed beads is an easy way to make bright, shiny eyes. Use glass seed beads (plastic beads may melt during baking.) Before placing eyes, mark their locations with a pin to judge the spacing. Place the bead at the end of the pin, then press the bead into the marking. Use the side of the pin to make a small indent in the clay on each side of the bead, giving the area shape.

Painted Eyes (after clay is baked): Make two large white dip dots (see inside the front cover) above the nose of each character. Let dry. Make a blue dip dot slightly above by overlapping the white dip dot. Let dry. Make a black dip dot slightly above and over lapping the blue dot. Let dry. Use a toothpick to make a white dip dot in the center of the black dip dot. Use the black pen to draw eyelashes and eyebrows around the eyes. Simple eyes are medium black dip dots with a tiny white dip dot in the center or to the side.

Fabriclay: Bond fabric to clay to support the fabric and strengthen the clay—translucent clay won't change the fabric color. This really requires a pasta machine—it's hard to get the clay thin enough with a hand roller. Roll the clay at the #1 setting, gradually increasing to #4. Lay the clay on the table and lay the fabric over it, right side up. Feed the fabric into the machine carefully so that it catches, roll at #6. Use scissors to cut the pattern shape. When attaching clay to the fabric side (such as a clay arm to a dress), secure with a small dab of tacky glue. (*Note*: Avoid using synthetic fabrics, as they may melt when baked.)

Hair: Use a garlic press or a KlayGun with a

medium multi-hole screen. Load with the specified clay color and squeeze out ¼" lengths of clay. Cut off with a knife. Use a toothpick to pick up clusters of hair and press to the head.

Making scallops: Make a scallop tool by cutting ½" of a plastic drinking straw in half lengthwise forming a half-circle. Cut a circle of the required width and use the scallop tool to cut away the edge of the clay. To create rows of scallops, use a scallop tool to cut away the edge of the clay. Use the tool ⅛" above the first row and indent for the second row of scallops. Use the side of the pin to indent the first row, making the second row seem raised or embossed.

Seal: A sealed project will have added shine and luster. Follow the manufacturer's directions to apply sealer to your project.

Rock 'n Roll by Sara Naumann

General Instructions: Condition the clay (see page 6) and roll it into a ball between the palms of your hands. Flatten the ball into a stone shape, place it on a flat surface and shape the edges. **To stamp on clay:** Ink the stamp with pigment ink and press gently into the unbaked clay. Use a baby wipe or soft cloth to remove ink smudges before baking.

Dream Rock

Granitex: ½" ball turquoise
"Dream" stamp (by Inkadinkado)
star cluster stamp (by Hero Arts)
gold pigment ink
½" wide gold moon charm
gold wire

Flatten the clay into a 2½" wide rock shape. Stamp the star cluster and "Dream" as shown. Bake. Thread the charm with the wire and wrap around the rock several times.

Four Variations

Sculpey®: gold
stamp by Inkadinkado

Granitex: violet
star cluster stamp by Hero Arts
purple metallic rub-ons

Granitex: brown
stamp by Inkadinkado

Granitex: brown
stamp by Inkadinkado

Terra Cotta Pot

Sculpey®: ¾" ball blue pearl
Granitex: ¾" ball black
1½" terra cotta pot
gold metallic paint
½" wide gold moon charm
gold E-bead
gold wire
skewer

Paint the pot gold, let dry. Blend the blue clay, working in small amounts of black with streaks of black showing throughout. Shape into a ¾" round disk and flatten. Poke a hole through the disk. Bake. Thread the moon charm onto the wire. Twist at the top to secure; add the bead, then wrap around the top of the pot as shown.

Inspire Domino

Sculpey®: 1" ball gold
"Inspire" stamp (by Inkadinkado)
black pigment ink
small gold dragonfly charm
gold wire
1½" domino
skewer

Wrap the clay around the domino. Stamp "Inspire". Gently press the charm into the clay. Bake. Add wire to the charm; curl as shown.

Dream Domino variation

Sculpey®: blue pearl
Granitex: black
"Dream" stamp (by Inkadinkado)

Eloisa Elephant by Judy Ferrill

Sculpey®: white, magenta, pink, ivory, black
2 black seed beads
round clay cutters: 5/16" and 3/16" (or use a plastic
* drinking straw and a coffee stirrer)*
#3 white perle cotton or heavy white carpet thread
four 1/4" wide white buttons with 2 holes
basic supplies (see inside the front cover)

actual height is 3"

First, blend to make:
• light gray: 1 package of black + 1/2 package
  of white

1 Body: Shape a 1 1/8" light gray ball into a 1 1/2" tall cone. Use a knife to draw a line down the center front and back, then turn the knife crosswise and use the tip to imprint stitches across the line as shown.
Head: Roll a 1" light gray ball and attach (see page 7) to her body. Imprint stitches as for the body. Press in the seed beads for eyes.

2 Ears: Flatten two 5/8" light gray balls to 1 1/4" across. Imprint stitches around the outer edge of each. Flatten two 1/2" pink balls to 1" across and attach one to the front of each ear. Use the knife to imprint five lines radiating as shown in the diagram. Pinch slightly at the base of each ear, trim off the pinched point and attach to the head as shown.

3 Trunk: Roll a 3/8"x1 1/8" light gray log. Use one finger to roll the center back and forth, thinning it slightly, then curve it to match the pattern. Attach one end to the bottom of the face, flaring it as you press it in place. Insert the handle of a paintbrush into the tip of the trunk and wiggle it to create a nostril opening. Repeat with a toothpick at the bottom base of the trunk to make the mouth. Imprint stitches along the center top and bottom of the trunk. **Tusks:** Roll two 3/8" ivory balls into cones and attach one to each side of the trunk as shown.

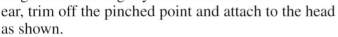

4 For each leg: Shape a 7/8" light gray ball to match the leg pattern. Pinch the top slightly to flatten it. Imprint stitches up the front, over the top and down the back. Flatten a 1/2" ivory ball to fit the bottom of the foot, then imprint stitches around the seam. Flatten magenta to 1/16" thick and cut three 5/16" circles. Imprint a 3/16" circle in the center of each. Use a toothpick to imprint button holes. Attach to the foot front. Pierce, bake and assemble (see inside the back cover).

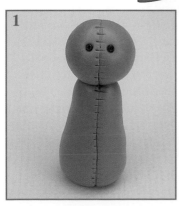

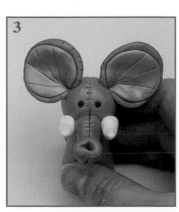

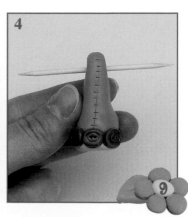

9

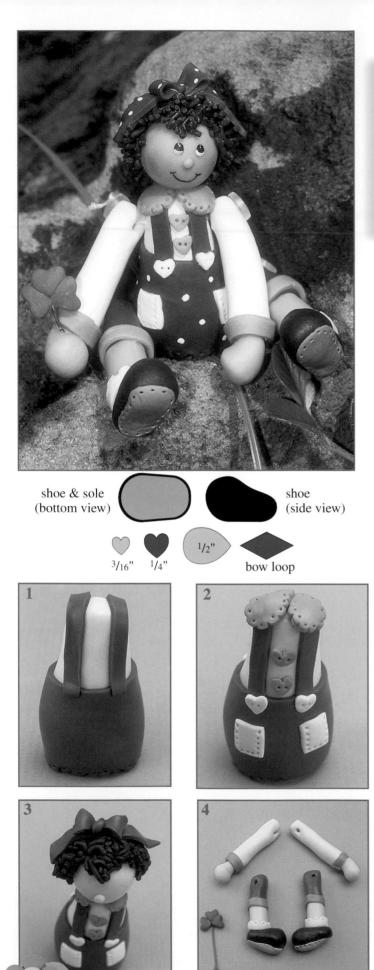

shoe & sole (bottom view)

shoe (side view)

3/16"   1/4"

1/2"

bow loop

1   2

3   4

top view

Sheilagh by Judy Ferrill

Sculpey®: beige, green, black, white, terra cotta, ivory
clay cutters: ³/16" and ¹/4" hearts, ¹/2" teardrop (or use the
*   patterns below)*
1¹/4" of 18-gauge wire
acrylic paint: black, white; #0 liner brush
pink powder blush, small paintbrush
#3 wide white perle cotton or heavy white carpet thread
four ¹/4" wide white buttons with 2 holes
garlic press or Kemper Klaygun
basic supplies (see inside the front cover)

First, blend to make:
• dark green: ¹/4 package of green + ⁹/16" ball of black
• light green: ¹/2" ball of green + ⁵/8" ball of white

1 **Body:** Shape a 1¹/8" white ball into a 1¹/2" tall cone. Flatten dark green to ¹/16" thick and cut a 3"x1" rectangle. Scallop (see page 7) one 3" and both 1" edges. Wrap around the cone with the 3" scalloped edge even with the bottom. **Suspenders:** Cut two ¹/8"x2" dark green strips and attach as shown.

2 Flatten white to ¹/16" and cut two ³/8" squares for pockets. Attach to the dress front. Cut four ³/16" hearts and attach for front and back suspender buttons. Flatten light green to ¹/16" thick. Cut two ³/16" hearts and attach between the suspenders for blouse buttons. Cut two teardrops, scallop each and attach as shown for her collar. Use the tip of a toothpick to imprint button holes and stitches around the pockets.

3 **Head:** Roll a ³/4" beige ball and attach it to her body. Roll a ¹/16" beige ball and attach for her nose. Make terra cotta hair. From the flattened dark green, cut two bow loops and a ¹/4"x1¹/2" strip for bow tails. Attach the tails to the top of her head. Fold the loops in half and attach the points to the center of the tails. Roll a ¹/8" dark green ball and press into the bow center for a knot.

4 **Arms:** Roll two ³/8"x1¹/2" white logs. Roll two ¹/2" beige balls into slightly oval hands and attach to the ends of the arms. From the flattened light green, cut two ¹/8"x1¹/4" strips and wrap for cuffs. **Legs:** Roll two ³/8"x⁵/8" dark green logs and two ³/8"x⁵/8" beige logs. Attach a beige log to the bottom of each green log. Make the cuffs as for the arms. From the flattened white cut two ¹/8"x1¹/4" strips. Scallop the top edges and wrap around the leg bottoms for socks. **Shoes:** Shape two ⁵/8" terra cotta balls into ovals and slightly flatten one end of each. Attach the flattened ends to the leg bottoms. Flatten two ¹/4" ivory balls into ovals and attach for soles; use a toothpick to imprint stitches around the soles. **Shamrock:** Cut three ¹/4" hearts from the flattened dark green. Attach in a triangle, points inward. Insert the wire into the shamrock and through one hand. Pierce, bake (see inside the back cover). Use the stylus or a toothpick to make white dip dots spaced evenly over the dress and bow. Assemble.

Belinda by Judy Ferrill

Sculpey®: white, pink, beige, turquoise, terra cotta,
* violet, green, yellow*
4" of 3/8" wide white scalloped flat lace
1 1/2" square of white ribbing fabric
needle, white thread
3/16" wide heart clay cutter (or use this pattern)
3/4" wide blue wicker basket
acrylic paint: black, white; #0 liner brush
pink powder blush, small paintbrush
#3 wide white perle cotton or heavy white carpet thread
four 1/4" wide white buttons with 2 holes
garlic press or Kemper Klaygun
artificial grass to fill basket
fine tip black marking pen
basic supplies (see inside the front cover)

1 **Body:** Shape a 1 1/8" white ball into a 1 3/8" tall cone. Wrap the lace around the cone with the scallops at the bottom and the ends at the back. **Skirt:** Flatten turquoise to 1/16" and cut a 3 1/4"x3/4" piece. Scallop (see page 7) the lower edge and both short edges. Wrap around the body so 1/4" of the lace shows. Imprint hearts around the lower edge. **Vest:** Flatten pink to 1/16" thick. Lay the pattern on the clay and cut around it. Wrap around the body, overlapping the skirt top. Join the ends and attach the shoulder straps in the back. Cut two 3/8"x1/4" pink strips and attach for pockets. Imprint a line down the center front. Roll a 1/16"x1" violet snake, cut four 1/4" lengths and attach over the front line, making two X's as shown for closures.

2 Roll a 3/4" beige ball and attach it to the body. Roll a 1/16" beige ball and attach for her nose. Make brown hair. **Bow:** From the flattened turquoise, cut two bow loops and two 1/8"x3/4" strips for tails. Attach the tails to the top of her head. Fold the loops in half and attach the points to the center of the tails. **Flower and Leaves:** Flatten two 1/8" green balls, shape each to a point and imprint a center line. Attach over the bow loops extending in opposite directions. Flatten two 1/16" violet balls and attach, slightly overlapping the leaves and each other. Repeat for three white petals, attaching the last over the first two. Roll a 1/16" yellow ball and place where the petals come together.

shoe   ♡   ◇ bow loop

3 **Arms:** Roll two 3/8"x1 3/8" white logs. Roll two 3/8" beige balls and attach one to the lower end of each log. **Legs:** Shape two 1/2" white balls into 5/8" tall cones. Roll two 1/4"x1" beige logs and attach one to the flat end of each cone. **Shoes:** Roll two 9/16" white balls into ovals, slightly flatten one end of each and attach the flattened ends at the bottoms of the legs. From the flattened pink cut two 1/4"x1/2" strips and attach over the shoes in front of the ankles. Make white laces as for the vest closures in step 1. Imprint stitch dots around the soles and gathers in the front of each shoe.

4 Pierce, bake, finish and assemble (see inside the back cover), but use the black pen to add a smile. **Socks:** Cut the ribbing into two 3/4"x1 1/2" strips with the ribs running crosswise. Wrap one around her ankle, turn the back edges under and sew. Repeat for the other leg. Secure the bottoms to the shoe backs with a dab of glue. Glue the basket into her hand.

1

2

back view

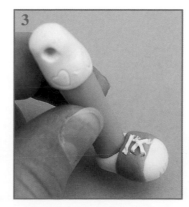

3

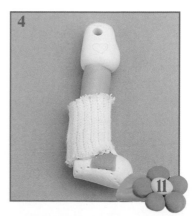

4

11

actual height 1¾" excluding antennae

Glory Bee by Shelly Comiskey

Sculpey®: white, gold, cadmium red, blue pearl
one 1½" long red metal miniature wagon
13" of 24-gauge black wire, wire cutters
clay cutters: ¾" teardrop, ⅜" star (or use these patterns)
2 size 15/0 black seed beads
⅛ tsp. of red embossing powder
pink chalk, 1" of white metallic yarn
basic supplies (see inside the front cover)

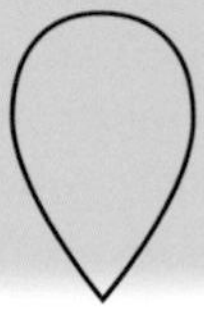

First, blend the embossing powder into a ¾" ball of white clay. In the following instructions, "white" refers to this blend.

1 **Body**: Shape a ⅝" gold ball into a pear. Flatten blue to ¹⁄₁₆" thick. Cut a ½"x2" strip and wrap around the body. Trim excess and smooth the seam in back. Flatten red to ¹⁄₁₆" thick and use the star cutter to cut a star. Press onto the body front. Glue the body bottom into the right wagon bed. Insert ⅓ of a toothpick into the body top so ¼" extends. **Head**: Shape an ¹¹⁄₁₆" gold ball into a rounded triangle; attach to the body top. Add a ³⁄₁₆" red ball for the nose and insert seed beads for the eyes. Use the straight pin to draw a smile and eyebrows. Bend two 1½" wire lengths as shown. Insert into the head top. Blush the cheeks.

2 **Wings**: Flatten white to ⅛" and use the teardrop cutter to cut two white wings. Attach one to each side of the top back. Cut two stars from the flattened blue; press one onto each wing front. Use the pin to poke two holes ½" apart in the body front as shown. Poke a hole in the center of each side.

3 **Flag**: Roll three red and two white logs, ⅛"x1½". Lay side by side, alternating colors. Flatten to ¹⁄₁₆". Cut a ¾"x1½" rectangle. Wrap ¼" of one short side around a 2½" wire length, pressing the edge down in the back. From the flattened blue, cut a ¼" square and attach to the upper left corner. From the flattened white,

cut a star and attach to the blue square. Ripple the flag as shown. **Hands**: Shape two ¼" white balls into teardrops and flatten slightly. Insert 1" wire lengths into the pointed ends. Fold one hand around the wire flagpole.

4 **Shoes**: Shape two ½" blue balls into tapered logs. Press the wide ends up and flatten the small ends. Pinch the heels into right angles. Flatten two ¼" white balls and press one onto the top of each shoe. Use the side of the pin to divide the soles from the heels. Press a ¹⁄₁₆" red ball onto each shoe front, then use the pin to poke two holes in each red ball. Glue a 1¼" wire length into the top of each shoe. **Firecrackers**: Roll a red, a white, and a blue log, each ⅛"x1". Twist together and roll to smooth. Roll to ⅛" thick. Cut a ½", a ¾" and a 1" length. Poke a hole in the top of each. Bake (see page 6) the bee, flag, hands, shoes and firecrackers. Let cool. Seal (see page 7).

(Refer to the large photo). Glue the leg and arm wires into the body holes. Bend the knees so the feet hang over the wagon. Glue the bottom of the flagpole inside the wagon. Fray the yarn. Glue small pieces into the tops of the firecrackers, then glue the firecrackers into the left wagon bed. Glue the remaining yarn into the wagon bed.

Ladybug by Shelly Comiskey

Sculpey®: black, translucent, red hot red, white
3" square of black/red polka-dot fabriclay (see page 7)
two 2" lengths of 24-gauge black wire
two 2" lengths of black perle cotton thread
red chalk
⅜" flower clay cutter (or use this pattern)
2 size 15/0 black seed beads
pink powder blush, small paintbrush
basic supplies (see inside the front cover)

actual height 3⅛" excluding antennae, with legs straight

1 **Body**: Shape a ⅞" black ball into a pear. Use the stylus to poke two holes ¼" apart in the bottom front. **Dress**: Cut a 2½" circle of fabriclay. Cut a slit from one side to the center, then wrap it around the body, overlapping the cut edges in the back. Glue to secure. Pinch and ruffle the dress into graceful folds. Insert ⅓ of a toothpick into the body top so ¼" extends. **Head**: Shape a ¾" black ball into a rounded triangle. Press onto the toothpick. Insert the seed beads for eyes. Attach a 3/16" red ball for the nose. Use the straight pin to draw a smile, eyebrows and an indent at the top of each eye. Blush the cheeks. Curl the wire ends as shown and insert into the top of the head.

2 **Arms**: Shape two ½" black balls into 1" long tapered logs. Slightly flatten the wide ends into hands. Glue the points to the shoulders, with her right hand extending upward in a wave and the left hand flattened onto the tabletop. **Necklace**: Roll five ⅛" white balls and use dots of glue to attach in a curve below the neckline of the dress.

3 **Shoes and socks**: Shape two ⅝" red balls into ovals and slightly flatten the back of each. Shape two 5/16" white balls into ovals, flatten and attach to the indented ends. Roll two ¼" white balls, flatten slightly and attach one to the back of each white oval. Roll a 1/16"x1" red rope, flatten and cut in half for the straps; attach one over the front of each white oval. Flatten white clay to 1/16" thick and use the flower cutter to

cut two flowers. Attach one to the top of each sock. Press a ⅛" black ball onto the outer end of each strap, indent with the stylus and poke two holes in each with the pin. Use the stylus to poke a hole in the top of each sock.

4 **Bow**: Cut the bow pattern below from fabriclay. Fold the ends to the back so they just meet and glue to secure. Press a ⅛" black ball into the bow center and use the pin to poke two holes in the ball. Bake (see page 6) the doll, bow and shoes. Let cool. Seal (see page 7). Knot each end of each thread length. Apply glue to the body front holes and the sock holes. Use the pin to push the knots into the holes, forming legs and attaching the shoes to the body as shown in the photo above. Let dry for 30 minutes.

bow pattern

13

this couple stands 2³/₄" tall

Happily Hitched
by Linda Welsh

Sculpey®: white, black, brown, tan, pale peach, translucent, burgundy, green, purple
four black seed beads
¹/₈" circle clay cutter
coffee stirrer
pink powder blush, small paintbrush
basic supplies (see inside the front cover)

First, blend to make:
• her hair: ⁷/₈" ball of translucent + ⁷/₁₆" ball of tan
• violet accents: ⁵/₁₆" ball of purple + ³/₁₆" ball of burgundy + ³/₁₆" ball of white

1 *For the Bride…* **Dress:** Shape a 1¹/₈" white ball into a 2" tall cone. Flatten white clay to ¹/₈" thick. Cut and scallop (see page 7) a 2³/₄" circle for her dress. Use the coffee stirrer to imprint each scallop and embellish with pin dots. Drape the dress, centered over the cone top, onto her body; use your thumb to smooth the dress downward and form ruffles as shown.

2 **Arms:** Roll two ⁹/₁₆" white balls into ³/₄" long tapered logs. Roll two ³/₈" peach balls and press to the wide ends for hands. Use the pin to indent fabric folds at her wrists as shown. Press to her body, bending her right arm slightly. **Shoulder ruffles:** Flatten white clay to ¹/₁₆" thick and cut a 1¹/₈" circle. Scallop the edges as for the dress in step 1. Cut the circle in half, gather each straight edge creating ruffles in the scalloped edge and press one ruffle to each shoulder, scalloped edges out. **Collar:** Cut a 1¹/₈" white circle. Scallop the edges as for her dress. Drape the collar over her shoulders. Insert a toothpick to extend ¹/₂" from her neck.

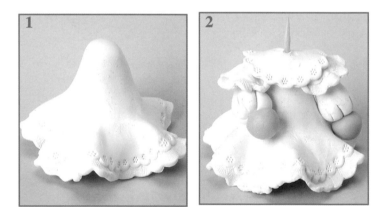

3 **Head and hair:** Roll a ³/₄" peach ball for her head and push onto the toothpick. Flatten a ¹/₂" hair color ball and press to the crown of her head. Shape two ¹/₂" hair color balls into tapered logs. Press the narrow ends to her head as shown and turn the ends up to curl. Roll three ³/₁₆"x¹/₄" hair color logs for bangs. Place as shown, curling the outer bangs outward. Press two seed beads below her bangs for eyes and use the pin to make lashes.

4 **Veil:** Flatten white clay to ¹/₁₆" thick for her veil. Cut a 1"x3" piece. Scallop and embellish one long edge as for her dress and collar. Place the corners of the straight side at each side of her head, press down then gather the back as shown. Roll a ¹/₈"x1¹/₂" white log, fashion it into a circle and place as shown.

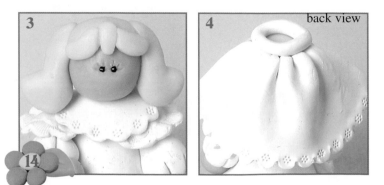

back view

14

5 **Rose buds:** Flatten a 3/16" white ball in your fingers; shape into a rectangle. Starting at one corner, roll to the other and pinch one end; trim the "stem" to leave only the bud. Make 12 of these. Press three evenly spaced to the crown of the veil and two on her dress collar. Mix equal amounts of green and white clay until they are marbled. Use a toothpick to shave tiny bits of this and violet clay, then press these shavings between the veil roses and sparsely around the outer edges of her right hand. Press the remaining roses among the green and violet shavings in her hand and on her collar. Roll three 1/16"x1/2" logs and press as bow tails extending from the bouquet as shown in the large photo on page 14.

6 ***For the Groom... Shoes and pants:*** Roll two 5/8" black balls and flatten to 1/2"x3/4" ovals for shoes. Roll two 5/16"x1" black logs. Insert a toothpick through the length of each, poke into each shoe's heel and set them close together as shown.

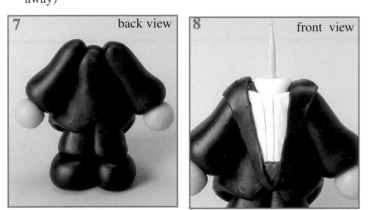

(cut this away)   tuxedo   tuxedo

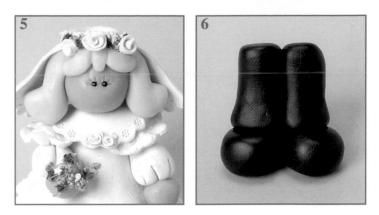

7 **Tuxedo:** Shape a 7/8" black ball into a cone. Use your thumb to indent the bottom, shaping the lower part of the cone to taper in the back. Use the knife to cut a 1/4" slit in the front middle and shape each side into points. Cut 1/2"x1/2" triangle from the back middle. Use your fingers to create a hollow in the tuxedo bottom to fit over his legs. Place on legs as shown. **Arms:** Roll two 5/8" black balls into 1" long tapered logs and press the narrow ends to his shoulders; roll two 3/8" peach balls and press to the wide ends for hands. Attach to his body.

8 **Tuxedo accents:** Flatten white clay to 1/16" thick and use the pattern to shape his shirt. Use a pin to draw two ruffle lines. Press to his chest. Flatten a 5/16" white ball to 1/16" thick and set on his neck for a collar. Shape a 5/16"x1/4"x1/16" violet rectangle for a cummerbund. Press to tuxedo just above the front slit. Use the collar patterns to cut his collar from 1/16" thick black clay. Press to overlap the shirt front and

cummerbund as shown. Insert a toothpick to extend 1/2" from his neck.

9 **Head:** Roll an 11/16" peach ball and push onto his neck. Flatten brown clay to 1/16" thick and cut a 1" circle. Press onto his head. Roll two 1/8" peach balls for ears, press one to each side of his head and poke each with the pin to define. Roll two 1/8"x1/2" brown logs and press as shown for bangs. Roll a 1/8"x1/4" log and curl over the center of his bangs. Press two seed beads for eyes and use the pin to indent lines.

10 **Bow tie:** Roll two 3/16" violet balls and slightly flatten each shaping them into triangles. Place them points together under his neck, using a pin to indent each. Press a 1/8" violet ball to the center, indenting it with the pin. Press a purple shaving and two green shavings to his lapel for a boutonniere. Cut two 1/4"x1/8"x1/16" black pieces, apply for pockets and indent each with a pin twice for buttons as shown in the large photo on page 14. Use the cutter to cut a black circle, indent for a button and place above the slit in his tuxedo back.

shirt front   lapels

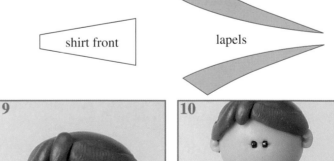

11 Press his right hand to her left hand. Carefully prop each onto a baking dish to prevent falling and bake (see page 6). Seal (see page 7).

15

actual height 1¾" excluding antennae

Garden Bug by Anita Behnen

Sculpey®: translucent, fluorescent green, yellow, sweet potato, maroon, raw sienna, black
1½" circle of beige/green fabriclay (see page 7)
one ¾" wide acorn cap
6–8 assorted dried miniflowers
two 3" lengths of 28-gauge black wire
black embossing powder
2 size 11/0 black seed beads
red chalk
clay cutters: ¾" heart, ⁵⁄₁₆" flower (or use the patterns above)
pink powder blush
small paintbrush
basic supplies (see inside the front cover)

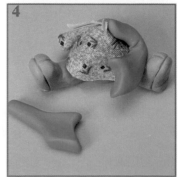

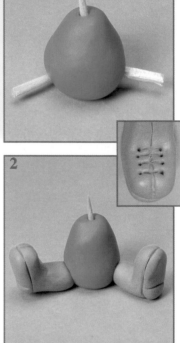

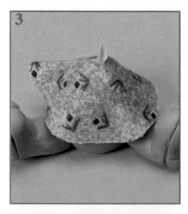

First blend to make:
• dark green: ¾" ball of fluorescent green clay + ½" ball of black clay
• gold: 1" ball of sweet potato + ⅞" ball of yellow + ⅝" ball of raw sienna

1 **Body**: Shape a ¾" dark green ball into an egg. Break a toothpick in thirds. Insert a piece into each side of the body base where the boots will be attached and one into the top of the body with ¼" extending.

2 **Boots**: Roll two ⁹⁄₁₆" gold balls into 1" long tapered logs. Bend each in half; pinch the bend to define the heel, then round the toe. Use the straight pin to score around each boot side just above the bottom to separate the sole. Press the side of the pin across the sole to create a heel. Draw a line along the center front and four shorter lines across it for laces. Poke four holes on each side for eyelets. Press one shoe onto each lower body toothpick.

3 **Dress**: Cut from one side of the fabriclay to the center. Wrap the fabriclay around the body as shown, overlapping the cut edges in the back. Secure with glue. Press the dress down around the body.

4 **Arms**: Shape two ½" dark green balls into 1" long tapered logs. Pinch the large end of each to flatten it into a half diamond. Pinch and pull the outer angle of the diamond to make a thumb. Roll the area just above the thumb between your thumb and forefinger to form a wrist. Bend the elbow. Apply glue to the inner top of each arm and press them onto the shoulders with the elbows touching the dress and boots. Be sure to leave enough room between the hands for the acorn cap.

5 **Head**: Shape a ½" dark green ball into an egg. Press a ¹⁄₁₆" dark green ball into the center for a nose. Insert the seed beads for eyes. Use the pin to draw a smile. Press the head onto the body top toothpick. Blush the cheeks and the tip of the nose.

hat

6 **Hat**: Flatten gold clay to ¹⁄₁₆" thick and cut a 1" circle. Place on the bug's head, pushing the edges down a little. Roll two ³⁄₈" gold balls. Flatten one and wrap it around the other, tucking the edges under. Press the tucked area into the center of the circle. Bend the front of the brim up.

7 Flatten maroon clay to ¹⁄₁₆" thick and use the flower cutter to cut a flower. Use the X-acto® knife to cut a 3-petal section. With the pin, draw 2–3 short lines extending from the center along each petal. Press the flower onto the turned-up area of the hat brim. Roll a ⅛" dark green ball into a ¹⁄₁₆" rope and wrap it under the cut edge of the flower.

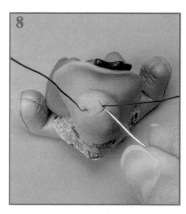

8 **Antennae**: Insert the two wire lengths into the top of the hat as shown. Use the pin to draw wrinkle lines radiating from the base of each antenna.

9 **Wings**: Flatten translucent clay to ¹⁄₁₆" thick and use the heart cutter to cut two wings. Use the pin to draw three lines on the front of each wing. Apply glue to her back shoulders and press the hearts into it, points almost touching. Roll a ⅛" dark green ball into a log and press over the wing points, connecting them. Use the pin to poke a hole in each end of the log.

10 **Basket**: Apply glue to the side of the acorn cap. Press the cap against the front of the dress. Apply glue to the inside of the bug's arms and press them around the back of the basket cap. Fold one thumb over the edge. Bake (see page 6), then seal (see page 7).

(Refer to the large photo on page 16.) Dip the antennae tips into glue, then into the jar of embossing powder. If you want a larger tip, let dry and repeat. After the powder has dried, bend the top third of each antenna down. Glue the dried flowers into the basket.

dress

actual height is 1¹/₂"

Patchwork Turtle
by Linda Welsh

*Sculpey®: green, magenta, yellow, brown,
   white*
two black seed beads
*clay cutters: ⁵/₁₆" heart, ⁵/₁₆" flower,
   ³/₁₆" teardrop, ³/₁₆" circle*
basic supplies (see inside the front cover)

First, blend to make:
• light yellow: ³/₈" yellow ball
  + ⁹/₁₆" white ball
• light green: ⁷/₁₆" green ball
  + ⁹/₁₆" white ball

front view   side view

1 **Legs:** Shape four ³/₈" green balls into ¹/₂" tall
cones. Place together as shown. **Head:** Roll a ⁹/₁₆"
green ball into a 1" log; round one end to shape it
as shown in the diagram and pinch the other end flat.
Press the flat end over the legs.

2 **Shell:** Shape an ¹¹/₁₆" brown ball into a cone;
round the top. Use the toothpick to indent shell
markings as shown. Press the shell over the legs and
bend the head back against it. Press the seed beads
in his face for eyes and use the pin to indent a smile
and lash lines.

3 **Neck Bow:** Flatten light yellow to ¹/₁₆" thick.
Cut two hearts; press them, points together,
below his neck. Use the pin to indent creases in the
bow. Press a ¹/₁₆" yellow ball to the bow center and
indent a crease in it. Make a ³/₈" square green and
light green patch (see page 63); press it to the shell.
Flatten yellow and magenta clay and cut a magenta
flower and a yellow circle. Press as shown; press a
¹/₁₆" white circle for a flower center and indent with
the pin. Use the pin to make two button holes in the
circle.

4 **Head bow:** Roll green clay to ¹/₁₆" thick; cut
two teardrops for leaves. Press to his head as
shown. Roll and press a ¹/₁₆" yellow and magenta ball
between the leaves and indent each. Bake (see page
6) then seal.

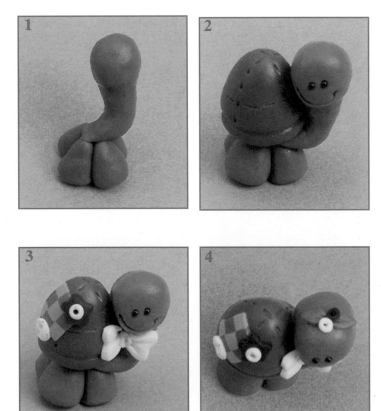

It's a Ladybug's Life
by Linda Welsh

Sculpey®: green, yellow, brown, red,
* black, white*
four 1" lengths of 24-gauge black wire
3" length of 24-gauge silver wire
two black seed beads
two black E-beads

5/16" teardrop clay
* cutter*
needle-nose pliers
basic supplies (see
* inside the front*
* cover)*

ladybug project is 2" tall

1 **Sunflower base:** Flatten green clay to 1/8" thick and use the pattern to cut out the maple leaf. Use the pin to draw the veins. Roll six 1/2" yellow balls into 5/8" long ovals; indent each with the toothpick and arrange as shown. Flatten a 7/16" brown ball into a 5/8" wide circle, poke "seeds" with the pin and press to the sunflower center.

2 **Large ladybug:** Roll a 5/8" red ball and flatten the bottom against the table top. Roll a 7/16" black ball and press for her head. Roll four 1/8" black balls and press for spots. Roll two 1/8" white balls and press as shown for eyes; press the E-beads into the base of the white balls. Press her to the sunflower as shown. Use the large antennae pattern and needle-nose pliers to shape her antennae from two 1" wire lengths. Insert as shown.

3 **Small flower:** Shape five 5/16" yellow balls into 3/8" long teardrops. Arrange the petals, points together, as shown and indent each petal with the toothpick. Flatten green clay to 1/16" thick, cut a 5/16" teardrop and press to extend from beneath the flower as shown.

4 **Small ladybug:** Roll a 5/16" red ball and flatten the bottom against the table top. Roll a 1/4" black ball and press for her head. Roll five 1/16" black balls and press for spots. Roll two 1/16" white balls and press as shown for eyes; press the seed beads into the base of the white balls. Press her to the sunflower and curl the petals downward as shown. Use the small antennae pattern and pliers to shape her antennae from two 1" wire lengths. Trim any excess and insert as shown. Coil the silver wire around the toothpick; insert one end into the small flower, passing through and into the ladybug, and the other end into the large flower. Bake (see page 6) and seal (see page 7).

19

project is 4" tall

Bathtub Buddies
by Shelly Comiskey

Sculpey®: white, pale peach, light blue
*   pearlescent, black*
many 2mm clear glass no-hole beads or seed
*   beads*
one 5" square of blue towel
jewelry glue (such as E-6000™ or Goop®)
2 black seed beads
2 blue seed beads
6" length of curly blond doll hair
pencil
pink chalk
small flat paintbrush
basic supplies (see inside the front cover)

1 **Tub legs:** Roll four 1" white balls into tapered logs. Indent the wide end of each with your thumb and taper the top as shown. Press two legs together, then place the pairs 1/4" apart. Use the pin to indent each foot twice.

2 **Tub basin:** Shape a 1 3/4" white ball into a 2" long by 1" wide oval dome, pressing the bottom flat against the table. Turn it over, flat side upward and press a hollow in the center about 3/8" deep. Press into the hollows of the legs, shaping the legs to hold the tub securely.

3 **Tub rim:** Roll a 7/8" white ball into a 7" long log. Flatten to 1/8" thick. Wrap around the top of the tub, pressing the ends together on one side.

4 **Water:** Flatten a 13/16" blue ball into an oval and press into the center of the tub. Gently press to fill the tub. Use a pencil to make two 3/8" wide holes in the top of the water.

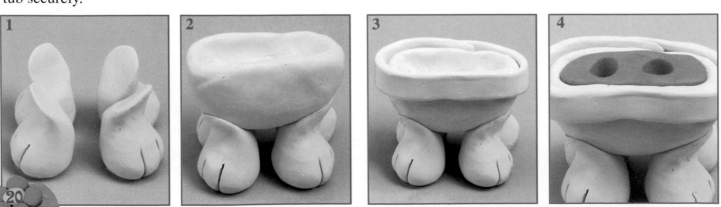

5 **Bodies:** Roll two ⁵⁄₈" peach balls into eggs. Press the small ends into the holes. Break a toothpick in half and insert one half into the top of each body, leaving ¹⁄₂" extending.

6 **Boy:** Shape a ³⁄₄" peach ball into a rounded triangle. Attach a ¹⁄₈" peach ball to each side of the head for ears and use the rounded end of the pin to indent. Press gently onto the left toothpick. Flatten a ⁹⁄₁₆" black ball to ¹⁄₄" thick. Cut a "V" in the front, then press onto the head, starting in the back and wrapping to the front. Roll two ¹⁄₈" black balls into teardrops and attach at the center top of his head for the cowlick. **Girl:** Shape a ⁷⁄₈" peach ball into a teardrop. Press the tip flat and to the back. Press gently onto the right toothpick. Be sure the heads are least ¹⁄₈" apart.

7 **Faces:** Insert two black seed beads (see page 7) for his eyes and two blue beads for hers. Use the pin to draw eyelashes and eyebrows above the eyes. Rub the paintbrush on the chalk, then use it to blush their cheeks. Shape a ¹⁄₂" blue ball into a rectangle for the soap. Bake (see page 6), then seal.

8 **Turban:** Cut the towel into a 2¹⁄₂"x1¹⁄₂" oval and a 2"x1" piece. Spread glue over the sides and top of her head. Wrap the oval towel around the head, starting in the front. Glue the overlapping edges together. Dab glue in the center of the 2"x1" towel piece and fold in half for the drying towel. Glue the soap to the center of the towel. Glue to the tub as shown.

9 **Hair:** Cut the doll hair into four 1" pieces. Glue three to the top of the turban and one crosswise for the bangs.

10 **Bubbles:** Spread glue inside the tub, letting some spill over the sides. Use a toothpick to spread some onto the soap. While the glue is wet, press the clear beads into the glue; let dry, then shake off the excess beads. Repeat if necessary.

turban

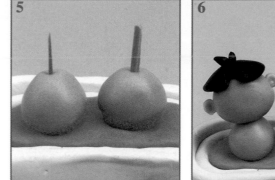

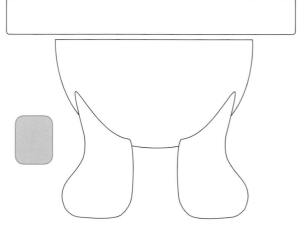

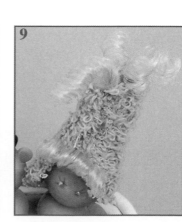

Noah stands 2³/8" tall.

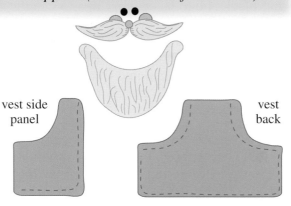

Noah by Linda Welsh

*Sculpey®: translucent, pale peach, gray,
brown, blue, burgundy, white, pink
2 black seed beads
3" length of 28-gauge silver wire
needle-nose pliers, dark brown acrylic paint
2" square of 120 grit sandpaper, soft cloth
basic supplies (see inside the front cover)*

vest side panel   vest back

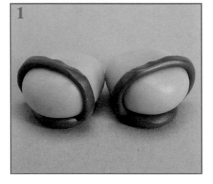

1 Sandals: Roll two ³/8" brown balls and flatten them each to ¹/8" thick ovals. **Feet:** Roll two ⁵/8" peach balls and flatten them each to ¹/4" thick ovals; press them onto his sandals. Roll two ¹/8"x1¹/4" brown logs and attach for sandal straps. **Ark:** Blend (see page 6) a ⁵/8" blue ball with a ⁵/8" gray ball. Use the patterns below to make the Ark; use the wire to poke a hole through each piece before baking. Set the Ark aside for step 4.

2 Body: Roll a 1¹/8" translucent ball into a 1⁷/16" tall cone. Indent with a pin for fabric folds as shown in the large photo. Press onto his feet. **Vest:** Flatten Ark gray clay to ¹/16" thick and use the patterns to cut out his vest. Cut two fronts and turn one over. Flatten a ¹/16"x3" gray log to ¹/16" thick; press to the vest bottom. Attach the vest as shown. Gently press the sandpaper over the vest to add texture then use the pin to make stitch lines and fringes.

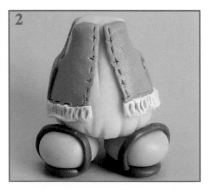

3 Arms: Shape two ¹/2" translucent balls into ³/4" long tapered logs. Press a ³/8" peach ball to each wide end for hands; use a pin to poke a hole into his left hand and to make fabric folds. Press the shoulders to his body. Use the pin to make an elbow crease in his left arm. Insert a toothpick into his neck to extend ¹/2". **Head:** Roll an ¹¹/16" peach ball; press onto the toothpick. Roll three ¹/8" pink balls; flatten two and press for cheeks, place the third for a mouth. Roll and place two ¹/8" peach balls for ears. Poke a pin into his mouth and ears to define each. Press in the seed beads for eyes.

4 Hair: Flatten a ⁷/16" white ball to ¹/16" thick. Shape the beard; place as shown in the large photo above. Shape two ¹/2" long white teardrops, press for a moustache with a ¹/8" peach ball for a nose. Cover each ear with a ¹/4" long white roll as shown. Shape and place two white ¹/8" teardrops for brows. Wrap a ¹/4" wide white strip around back from ear to ear. Bake. Thread wire through his hand and the Ark. Use pliers to coil and bend ends to secure. Antique the project then seal (see page 7).

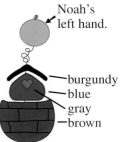

Noah's left hand.

— burgundy
— blue
— gray
— brown

All Ark pieces except the heart are ¹/4" deep.

Noah's Ark by Linda Welsh

Sculpey®: blue, green, gray, peach,
* burgundy, translucent, orange, black, brown*
8" length of 28-gauge black wire
ten black seed beads, unsharpened pencil
clay cutters: 1/2" circle, 3/8" heart
pink chalk, small paintbrush
basic supplies (see inside the front cover)

Noah's Ark is 4" tall.

house heart

trunk

1 **Ark:** Shape a 1 3/4" blue ball into a 3"x1 5/8"x1 1/2" boat; taper the ends as shown and press the bottom flat. Use the pin to make cross hatch lines for wood. Roll a 1/8"x12" blue log; fold it in half and twist. Press along Ark rim. **House:** Shape a 1" translucent ball into a rounded triangle; square the sides. Flatten a 7/8" burgundy ball to 1/4" thick; place for a roof. Flatten green clay to 1/16" thick and use the cutter to cut a heart. Press to the house and poke two button holes with the pin. Press in ark center. Use the cutter to make four green circles. Indent each with the pencil. Poke each twice with a pin for button holes and press to the Ark for wheels.

2 ***Giraffes…* Bodies:** Roll two 1/4"x1 3/4" peach logs. Insert a toothpick into each body and insert into the Ark. **Feet:** Roll four 1/4"x1/2" peach logs; taper one end on each. Press two legs to extend from each body. **Heads:** Shape two 9/16" peach balls into teardrops. Press a head to each body. **Ears:** Shape four 5/16" peach balls into 1/2" long tapered logs and form to each head. **Spots:** Flatten many 1/16"-1/8" brown balls between your fingers; apply to body parts as shown. **Hooves:** Flatten and press a 5/16" brown ball to each foot bottom. **Antlers:** Cut four 1/2" lengths of wire, insert two into each head and push a 1/4" brown ball onto each. Use the pin head to indent nostrils; press two seed beads for eyes into each face and use the pin to indent brows.

3 ***Elephants…* Legs:** Shape four 1/2" gray balls into 3/4" long tapered logs; press to drape over the Ark rim as shown. **Heads:** Shape two 9/16" gray balls into rounded triangles and press one over each pair of legs. **Ears:** Flatten four 3/8" gray balls between your fingers, pinch the side and create a cupped elephant ear shape. Press two to each head. **Trunks:** Roll two 3/8" gray balls into 3/4" long logs, curve each into a loose "S", press to the faces and press two seed beads for eyes.

4 ***Bird…* Body:** Shape a 1 1/4" black ball into a 3/4" tall teardrop, insert a toothpick into the neck to extend from both ends and press onto Ark house. **Feet:** Flatten two 1/4" orange balls into teardrops, indent each twice for toes and press to the body bottom. **Wings:** Shape two 5/8" black balls into tapered logs and press the narrow ends to the shoulders. **Head:** Shape a 9/16" black ball into a teardrop, pull and curl the tip for hair and place the head on the toothpick. Shape a 1/8" long orange triangle for a beak and press it and two seed beads for eyes into his face. Blush the cheeks of the giraffes and elephants with the paintbrush and chalk as shown in the large photo. Bake (see page 6) then seal (see page 7).

project stands 2¼" tall.

Country Horse
by Linda Welsh

Sculpey®: tan, red, blue, yellow, brown, black
¼"x3" strip of burgundy checked fabric
two black seed beads
black Lil' Loopies® hair
¼" star clay cutter
coffee stirrer
pink powder blush, small paintbrush
basic supplies (see inside the front cover)

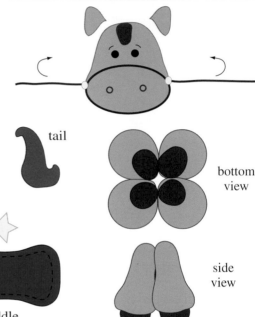

tail

bottom view

side view

saddle

1 **Legs:** Roll four ⁹⁄₁₆" tan balls into ³⁄₄" long tapered logs. Press together as shown. **Hooves:** Roll a ³⁄₈"x³⁄₄" brown log. Cut four ³⁄₁₆" pieces and press one hoof to the bottom of each leg. **Body:** Flatten a ⁷⁄₈" tan ball slightly between your fingers and press on top of the legs. Insert a toothpick to angle ½" outward from his neck.

2 **Head:** Shape an ¹¹⁄₁₆" tan ball into a rounded triangle; press onto the toothpick. **Spots:** Flatten two ¹⁄₈" black balls and four ¼" brown balls. Press to legs, head and body as shown. **Ears:** Shape two ⁵⁄₁₆" tan balls into cones and attach as shown. Use the stirrer to indent his nose; press seed beads for eyes and use the pin to draw brows as shown. **Tail:** Shape a ³⁄₈" brown ball into a ³⁄₄" long log. Curl each end and press to his hind end as shown.

3 **Saddle:** Flatten blue clay to ¹⁄₁₆" and use the pattern to make a saddle. Make stitch lines with the pin and press it over his back curling the back edge up for a seat. Cut a ¹⁄₁₆" thick yellow star; roll a ¹⁄₈"x½" blue log, fold and place for stirrup; secure with the star.

4 **Bridle:** Roll red clay into a ¹⁄₁₆"x4" log. Cut 2" and wrap it around his nose; wrap the remaining around his neck and trim any excess. Poke 2 holes along his neck for mane and blush his muzzle. Bake (see page 6); seal (see page 7). Use the fabric to make a collar bow; glue it under his neck as shown. Use the Loopies® hair to make two poms each with many loops. Apply glue to the wire ends and insert into his mane holes.

Button Bunny by Judy Ferrill

Sculpey®: white, turquoise, lavender, yellow, pink
³/₁₆" heart clay cutter (or use the pattern on the vest)
3" square of unbleached muslin fabric
fabric stiffener
³/₄" square of gold foil paper
1 gold seed bead
acrylic paint: black, white; #0 liner brush
pink powder blush, small paintbrush
#3 wide white perle cotton or heavy white carpet thread
four ¹/₄" wide white buttons with 2 holes
basic supplies (see inside the front cover)

ear

foot

1 Trace the patterns and cut out. **Ears:** Cut two ears from muslin. Dip in fabric stiffener, squeeze out excess and shape the ears as desired; pinch the bases. Place on waxed paper to dry; set aside for step 2. **Body:** Shape a 1¹/₈" white ball into a 1¹/₂" long cone. **Pants:** Flatten turquoise to ¹/₁₆" thick and cut a 3"x1¹/₂" rectangle. Wrap around the body so ¹/₂" extends below. Fold under and smooth. Use your finger to indent the lower front. Cut two ³/₈"x¹/₄" turquoise pieces and attach for pockets; use a toothpick to make stitching dots. **Vest:** Flatten lavender to ¹/₁₆" thick. Lay the pattern on the clay and cut around it. Wrap around the body, overlapping the pants and pocket tops. Join the ends and attach the shoulder straps in the back. Indent a line down the center front. Make lavender pockets as for the pants. From the flattened turquoise cut a single heart and attach for a button. Imprint button holes.

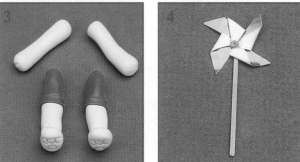

2 **Head:** Roll a ³/₄" white ball and follow the general directions to attach. Flatten a ¹/₄" white ball into an oval and attach for the muzzle. Draw a slit down the center. Attach a ¹/₈" pink ball for the nose. **Hat:** Flatten a ⁵/₈" yellow ball to 1" across and attach to the top of the head. Flatten a ¹/₂" yellow ball to ³/₄" across and attach for the brim. Draw lines on the hat to simulate woven straw. Roll a ¹/₁₆"x3" lavender rope, wrap for a hat band and trim excess. Insert the ears into the hat as shown. Blush the inner ears.

3 **Arms:** Roll two ³/₈"x1³/₄" white logs; slightly flatten one end of each. Imprint toe slits on the rounded ends. **Legs:** Roll two ³/₈"x1" turquoise logs. Roll two ³/₈"x1¹/₄" white logs and attach one end to the end of each turquoise log. Turn up ⁵/₈" on the other end. Imprint paw pads with the heart cutter, or draw pads with the toothpick. From the flattened turquoise cut two ¹/₄"x1" strips and wrap one around each leg between the blue and white for a cuff.

4 Pierce, bake, finish and assemble (see inside the back cover). **Pinwheel:** Fold the paper square in fourths. Cut from the open corner diagonally ³/₄ of the way to the opposite corner. Open up the paper. Fold alternate corners into the center, securing with glue. Glue the bead into the center. Cut a toothpick in half and glue the pinwheel to one end. Glue to the bunny's hand.

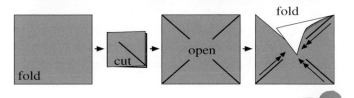

fold

fold   cut   open   fold

Spring Bunny
by Shelly Comiskey

actual height is 3¹/₄" tall.

Sculpey®: white, yellow,
   green, stone-look green,
   stone-look blue,
   stone-look pink,
   stone-look purple
2 black glass seed beads
4¹/₂" of 4-lb.
   monofilament nylon
   fishing line
tweezers
basic supplies (see inside
   the front cover)

First, blend to make:
• grass: 1¹/₄" stone-look
   green ball + ³/₈" green ball
   + ³/₄" white ball

1 Flatten a 1¹/₄" grass-colored ball to ³/₈" thick and shape to match the base pattern on page 27. **Legs:** Shape two ³/₄" white balls into tapered logs. Indent the wide end of each with your thumb. Press the legs together in the center of the base. Insert a ³/₄" long toothpick into each, extending ¹/₂". Use the pin to make two toe lines at the bottom of each foot.

2 **Body:** Shape a 1¹/₈" white ball into a pear. Press onto the leg toothpicks, centering so the figure stands balanced. Insert a ¹/₄" long toothpick into the top of the body, leaving ¹/₈" extending.

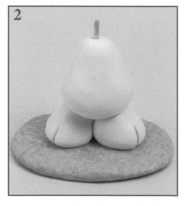

3 **Arms:** Shape two $^{11}/_{16}$" white balls into tapered logs, rounding off the wide ends. Attach the small ends at the shoulders. Rest the arms on the tummy, meeting in front as shown. Use the pin to make two toe lines at the end of each arm.

4 **Head:** Shape a 1" white ball into a rounded triangle. Press gently onto the neck toothpick. Shape two $^7/_{16}$" white balls into teardrops for ears. Flatten to $^1/_8$" thick. Roll two $^1/_4$" pink balls into $^1/_2$" long ovals and flatten to $^1/_{16}$" thick. Attach one to the center of each ear. Attach the ears to the top back of the head, curving the tips inward as shown.

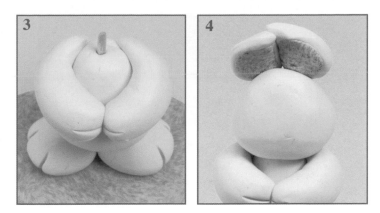

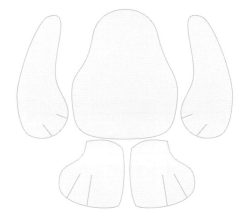

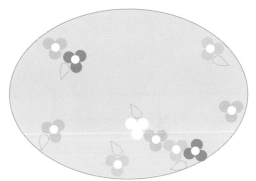

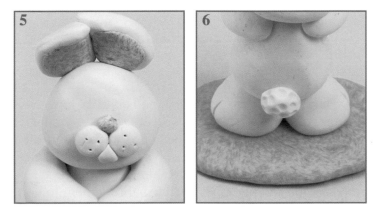

5 **Muzzle:** Flatten two $^1/_4$" white balls. Press side by side onto the lower half of the face. Use the pin to make three dots in each muzzle. Flatten a $^1/_8$" white ball and attach it underneath the muzzle. Flatten a $^1/_8$" pink ball and attach it to the top of the muzzle.

6 **Eyes:** Insert the seed beads (see page 7) for eyes. Use the pin to draw eyelashes and eyebrows above the eyes. **Whiskers:** Cut six $^3/_4$" long pieces of fishing line. Use the tweezers to insert three into each side of the muzzle. **Tail:** Attach a $^3/_8$" white ball to the lower back. Use the rounded end of the pin to imprint curls all over the tail.

7 **For each flower:** Place three $^1/_8$" balls of the same color (pink, blue, purple, or yellow) together and flatten slightly. Press the center with the rounded end of the pin. Add a $^1/_{16}$" white ball to the center of each flower. Make a total of 12 flowers, varying the colors.

8 **For each leaf:** Flatten a $^3/_{16}$" grass-colored ball and shape to match the pattern. Make ten leaves. Attach a leaf and flower to her arms and two leaves and a flower next to her left ear as shown. Attach the remaining leaves and flowers to the base as shown in the pattern. Bake (see page 6), then seal.

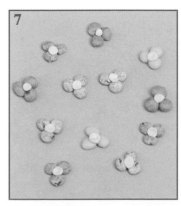

Bunny sits 3½" tall

Patchwork Bunny
by Linda Welsh

Sculpey®: pale peach, green, white, blue, burgundy, gray
two black seed beads
clay cutters: 5/16" square, 3/16" circle, 7/8" heart
pink chalk, small paintbrush
dark brown acrylic paint, soft cloth, coffee stirrer
basic supplies (see inside the front cover)

First, blend to make:
• patch-green: 5/8" green ball + 7/16" white ball
• patch-blue: 1½" blue ball + 7/8" gray ball
• patch-pink: 3/8" burgundy ball + 3/4" white ball
  + 1" peach ball

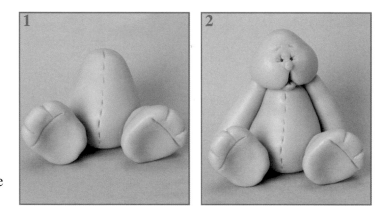

1 **Body:** Shape a 1⅛" ball of peach into a 1¼" tall cone; use your fingers to round the front to plump her tummy. Use the pin to draw stitches down her tummy. **Legs:** Shape a 3/4" peach ball into a tapered log; use your fingers to shape the wide end into an oval foot. Repeat for the other leg. Attach the legs. Use your thumb to indent the soles of her feet; use the pin to indent the balls and to make toe lines.

2 **Arms:** Shape two 11/16" peach balls into 1½" long tapered logs; press the narrow ends to each shoulder. Insert a toothpick to extend ½" from her neck. **Head:** Shape a 7/8" peach ball into a rounded triangle; use the knife to cut a slit in the bottom center. Use your fingers to round the muzzle. Roll and insert a 3/16" pink ball for a mouth then close the slit. Press a 1/16" pink ball at the muzzle top for a nose; press the seed beads for eyes and make lashes and brows with the pin. Push her head onto the toothpick. Use the pin to poke a hole in her mouth and define the muzzle.

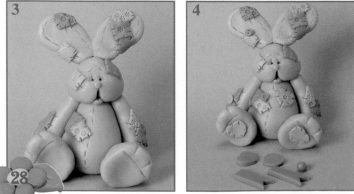

3 **Ears:** Shape two 5/8" peach balls into 1" long tapered logs; flatten and curve. Draw stitch lines with the pin and press to her head as shown. **Patches:** Roll the green, pink and blue clays to 1/16" thick each. Use the square cutter to cut five blue patches, three green patches and five pink patches. Press them to her body as shown using the pin to make stitch lines and to poke dot patterns on each patch.

4 **Accents:** Use the circle cutter to cut four green and one pink button; poke each with the pin for button holes and place as shown. Use the heart cutter to cut two blue and three pink hearts. Press the pink hearts into her foot bottoms and body adding stitch marks with the pin. Press the blue hearts, tips together, to her forehead. Press a 1/8" blue ball to the center, indent with the pin. Cut two 1/4"x3/4" blue strips, cut one end on each into an inverted "V" and tuck the other end under each side of the bow as shown. Blush the cheeks with the chalk and paintbrush. Bake (see page 6) and antique, then seal (see page 7).

Easter Bunny
by Shohreh Dolkhani

actual width 3¼"

Sculpey®: white, pink, lavender, yellow,
*   orange, green, red*
floral moss
cardboard: 3¼"x2¼" piece, 1¾"x1" piece
stiff toothbrush
pink powder blush, small paintbrush
acrylic paints: light blue, black, white
#0 liner paintbrush
broad-tip black permanent pen
basic supplies (see inside the front cover)

1 Legs: Shape two ¹¹/₁₆" white balls into 1" long tapered logs. Indent the wide end of each with your thumb. **Body:** Shape a 1" white ball into a cone and press onto the legs. Push a ½" length of toothpick into the top, leaving ¼" exposed. **Tail:** Shape a ⁷/₁₆" white ball into a teardrop. Press onto the lower back.

2 Arms: Shape two ½" white balls into tapered logs. Press one onto each side of the body. **Head:** Shape a ¾" white ball into an egg. Press onto the toothpick. **Ears:** Push two ½" toothpick lengths into the head, leaving ¼" of each exposed. Flatten two ½" white balls into long ovals. Blush the inner ears, cheeks and tummy. Pinch the bottom of each each, then press one onto each toothpick. Tilt the ear tips forward. Use a pin head to poke a hole in the tummy.

3 Paw pads: Flatten two ¼" and six ³/₁₆" pink balls. Press onto the bottoms of the feet as shown. **Nose:** Shape a ³/₁₆" pink ball into a rounded triangle. Press onto the face. Use the pin to draw a muzzle line under the nose and three whisker dots on each cheek. **Collar:** Wrap a ¹/₁₆"x2" lavender log around the neck. **Bow:** Flatten lavender to ¹/₁₆" thick and cut two ¼"x1¼" strips. Cut one in half, then trim one end

of each half in an inverted "V". Attach to the collar as shown. Pinch the center of the other length, then pinch each end and fold the ends to the center, forming a bow. Attach to the tops of the tails.

4 Chick: Shape a ³/₈" yellow ball into a rounded triangle. Shape two ³/₁₆" yellow balls into teardrops and attach for wings. Shape a ¹/₈" orange ball into a cone and attach for a beak. Attach the chick to the bunny as shown in the large photo above. **Eggs:** Mix together red, green, and yellow (you can also use scraps), making a marbled clay—don't overblend! Shape five ⁵/₁₆" balls into eggs. Arrange the eggs in a pile. Bake (see page 6). Paint eyes (see page 7) on the bunny and simple eyes on the chick. **Sign:** Spatter (see inside the back cover) the cardboard with white, then with black paint. Use the broad-tip pen to write "Happy Easter" on the cardboard. Make black dip dots on the ends of the letters. **Base:** Glue moss to cover the large piece of cardboard. Glue the bunny, eggs and sign into the moss as shown in the large photo.

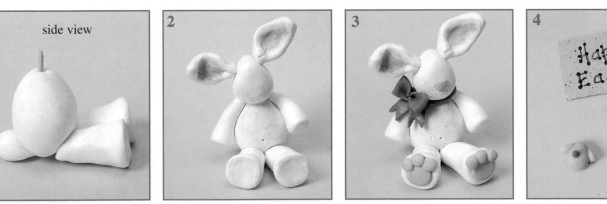

1 side view

2

3

4

29

Garden Glove Bunny
by Linda Welsh

including the glove, this garden bunny is 5¹/₂" tall.

Sculpey®: stone-look blue, pale peach, red, white, orange, yellow, green, brown, tan
3¹/₂" long miniature gardening glove
¹/₂"x³/₈" piece of burgundy printfabric
¹/₂" square of blue checked fabric
1 skein green embroidery floss
green excelsior
"Plant seeds of love" rubber stamp
clay cutters: ⁵/₁₆" flower, ⁵/₁₆" teardrop,
    ³/₁₆" heart,
    ³/₁₆" circle
two black seed beads
dark brown acrylic paint
pink powder blush, small paintbrush
soft cloth
18" length of 22-gauge wire
wire cutters
basic supplies (see inside the front cover)

1 Body: Shape a 1" stone-look blue ball into a 1¹/₂" tall cone. Flatten slightly. **Arms:** Shape two ⁹/₁₆" red balls into 1" long tapered logs and press two ⁷/₁₆" white balls on the wide ends for hands. Use the pin to indent finger lines. Press a shoulder to each side of his body leaving a gap between his lower arms and body. Insert a toothpick into the neck to extend ¹/₂".

2 Overalls: Flatten a ¹/₂" stone-look blue ball to ¹/₁₆". Cut two ³/₁₆"x1" strips for straps, two ¹/₄" squares for patches and one ¹/₂"x³/₈" rectangle for a pocket; flatten a green, a red and an orange scrap to ¹/₁₆" thick and use the clay cutter to cut one green, two red and one orange buttons. Press the pocket, patches and straps in place, press on the buttons and make stitch marks and button holes with a pin as shown.

3 Head: Shape a 7/8" peach ball into a rounded triangle. Use the knife to cut the muzzle as shown in the pattern. Press onto the toothpick. Roll and flatten a 1/8" pink ball; press at base of his muzzle for a tongue. Roll a 1/16" pink ball; press above the muzzle line for his nose. Press seed beads above his nose for eyes and use the pin to make lashes and brows as shown. **Ears:** Flatten two 5/8" peach balls into 1 1/4" long teardrops. Use the pin to draw stitch lines on his ears and face. Press an ear to each side of his head. Use the paintbrush and chalk to blush his cheeks and inner ears.

4 Hat: Flatten brown clay to 1/8" thick and cut a 1 3/4" circle for a brim. Place it on the back of his head folding the front up as shown. Shape an 11/16" brown ball into a cylinder and indent the top with your thumb. Press the cylinder to the hat top, behind the brim fold as shown. Use a toothpick to make cross hatch marks and tatters. **Flowers:** Roll yellow and green scraps to 1/16" thick. Cut three yellow flowers; cut two green leaves. Press a 1/8" orange ball to each flower center. Press the leaves and two flowers to the hat brim as shown. Set aside the third flower for step 6.

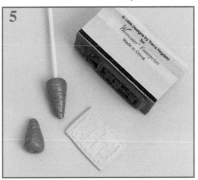

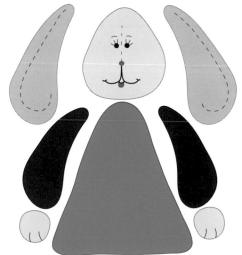

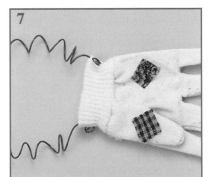

5 Carrots: Shape two 7/16" orange balls into 3/4" long cones and imprint lines with the pin. Use the toothpick to poke a hole 1/8" deep into the tops of each carrot. Flatten tan clay to 1/8" thick. Push the rubber stamp into the clay and cut around the imprint cutting off the hanger. Bake all pieces (see page 6).

6 Antique (page 7) the Bunny, his carrots, the flowers and plaque and seal. Use the green floss to make two poms, each with twelve loops—don't cut the loops; set aside for step 8.

7 Coil the wire around the paintbrush handle. Remove and poke 1/2" of one end into the thumb side of the glove, 1/4" below top. Bend upward and coil the end to secure. Repeat for other end on the pinky side. Glue the fabric patches to the glove palm as shown.

8 Glue the remaining flower to blue checked patch. Glue the stamped plaque as shown in the large photo on page 30. Glue and insert the carrot tops into the carrot holes; glue them to glove as shown. Stuff the glove with excelsior grass. Slip Bunny into the glove opening and glue his hands to the glove to secure. Glue a few more strands of the excelsior grass around Bunny as shown in the large photo on page 30.

actual height is 3³/₄"

Fireman & His Dog
by Linda Welsh

Sculpey®: yellow, red, white, black, pale peach, ecru
2 blue seed beads
2 black seed beads
pink chalk, small paintbrush
black fine-tip permanent-ink pen
³/₈" heart clay cutter
basic supplies (see inside the front cover)

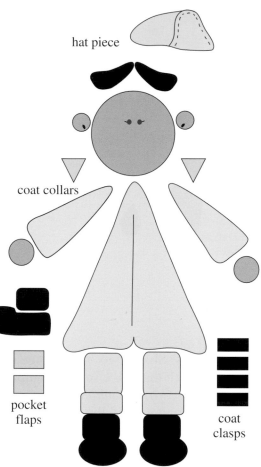

hat piece

coat collars

pocket flaps

coat clasps

1 *For the Fireman…* **Boots:** Flatten two ⁵/₈" black balls to ¹/₂"x⁷/₈" ovals, thicker at the front. Add a slightly flattened ¹/₂" black ball over each heel for boot legs; push a toothpick into the top of each and trim so ¹/₂" extends. Use a toothpick to poke four lacing holes up each boot side. **Legs:** Roll two ¹/₂"x³/₄" yellow logs and push one onto each toothpick. Cut two ¹/₄"x1"x¹/₁₆" yellow strips. Wrap each around the lower leg for pant cuffs; trim off excess. Set the legs side by side.

2 **Coat:** Shape a 1" yellow ball into a 1³/₈" tall cone. Use your thumb to indent the bottom. Cut a shallow slit down the front of the coat and press over the legs. Flatten yellow clay to ¹/₁₆" thick; use the patterns to cut 2 coat collars and 2 pocket flaps. Flatten black clay to ¹/₁₆" thick; use the pattern to cut 4 coat clasps. Attach the collars to the neck of the coat, the pocket flaps at the waist and the coat clasps down the front as shown. **Arms:** Shape two ¹¹/₁₆" yellow balls into 1" long tapered logs. Press a ³/₈" peach ball to the wide ends for hands. Press one to each shoulder. Insert a toothpick in his neck to extend ¹/₂".

3 **Head:** Press a ³/₄" peach ball onto his neck. Roll two ¹/₈" peach balls, indent the front of each with the pin and press one to each side of his head. Press the blue seed beads into his face for eyes; use the pin to make a smile line by each. Use the paintbrush and chalk to blush his cheeks.

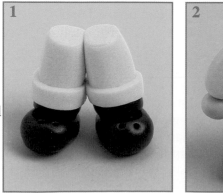

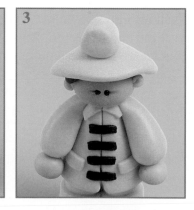

32

Hair: Flatten a 1/2" black ball to a 1" circle. Press to the top of his head. Shape two 5/16" black balls into flattened teardrops; press each, points in the middle and overlapping his hair, to his forehead for bangs. **Hat:** Flatten a 7/8" yellow ball into a 1 1/2"x1 3/4" oval; lay over his hair. Roll a 5/8" yellow ball into a 7/8" long tapered log. Lay the log, wide end forward, on his hat brim as shown.

4 *For the Dalmatian…*
Body: Shape a 7/8" white ball into a rounded triangle. Use the knife to cut a 1/2" slit up the center. Insert a toothpick into his neck to extend 1/2". **Legs:** Roll two 5/16" white balls and press one at the base of each front leg. Shape two 9/16" white balls into 1/2" tall cones. Lie each to extend wide ends forward. Slightly indent the bottom of each with your thumb and use the the knife to cut two toe lines. **Head:** Shape a 3/4" white ball into a rounded triangle. Slightly flatten a 1/4" white ball and use the knife to cut a slit half way up the center. Press this to the lower front of the head for a muzzle. Roll a 1/16" black ball; press for a nose as shown. Poke a mouth hole under the muzzle with a toothpick. Push his head onto his neck.

5 **Ears:** Shape two 7/16" white balls into teardrops and press to his head as shown. **Spots:** Flatten many 1/16"-3/16" black balls. Place on his body, head and ears as shown. Press a 3/16" flattened black ball above the muzzle and left for an eye patch. Press two black seed beads above the muzzle for eyes. Use a tiny piece of red clay to tuck into his mouth for a tongue. Use the paintbrush and chalk to blush his cheeks.

6 **Tail:** Shape a 3/16"x7/8" white log and attach to his rear. **Pads:** Press a 3/16" flattened black ball with three 1/16" flattened black balls to the bottom of each rear foot. **Collar:** Roll a 1/16"x2" red rope; wrap around his neck. Flatten a

3/8" red ball to 1/16" thick and cut out two hearts. Place them, points together, at his left collar for a bow. Use the pin to press a 1/8" red ball to the bow center, and to make a crease line in each heart center.

7 *For the Fire Hydrant:*
Shape a 3/4"x1" red cylinder. Make vertical lines with the pin. Roll a 1/2"x1/2" tall red cone. Press onto the cylinder top and continue the pin lines to the top. Flatten a 3/4" red ball to 1/16" thick. Cut a 2 1/2"x1/4" strip, wrap it around the bottom of the hydrant and trim excess; cut a 2 1/2"x3/16" strip, wrap it around the upper part of the hydrant and trim excess. Make vertical lines with the pin. Flatten three 5/16" red balls and place on the front, left and right sides as shown. Slightly flatten two red 1/8" balls; press on left and right hydrant valves. Place a 3/16" red ball on the hydrant top.

8 *For the fire hose:* Roll a 3/4" tan ball to a 1/16"x5" log. Fold in half and twist together. Press one end to the hydrant front, loop the hose and place the other end in his left hand. Shape a 5/16" black ball into a 1/2" tapered log. Place it over the left hose end for a nozzle. Roll a 1/4"x1/16" log for a nozzle valve as shown. Bake (see page 6). Draw dashed lines with the pen around his hat then seal (see page 7).

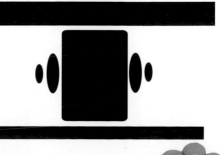

Mickey is 3¹/₂" tall, his dog is 1³/₄"

Mickey by Shelly Comiskey

Sculpey®: *stone-look blue, stone-look brown, stone-look green, pale peach, light brown, green, yellow, white, black*
6 black glass seed beads
basic supplies (see inside the front cover)

First, blend to make:
• light blue: ⁵/₈" white ball + ³/₈" stone-look blue ball
• light green: ¹/₄" white ball + ³/₁₆" green ball

1 **Boy—shoes:** Flatten two ⁹/₁₆" white balls to ¹/₈" thick ovals for soles. Use the pattern to shape two ¹³/₁₆" black balls. Attach to the top of the soles. Flatten two ⁵/₁₆" white balls and press one onto the front of each shoe. Attach them side by side as shown. Press a ¹/₈" white ball onto the inside of each shoe.

2 **Cuffs:** Flatten two ⁹/₁₆" light blue balls to ³/₁₆" thick. Attach one to the top of each shoe. Push a ¹/₂" long toothpick into the center top of each cuff, angled slightly inward. **Body:** Shape a 1³/₈" stone-look blue ball into an egg. Press the wide end onto the toothpicks at the tops of the cuffs; be sure he balances. Flatten a ¹/₄" stone-look blue ball to ¹/₁₆" thick. Cut into a ³/₈" square and attach to the front of the body. Use the pin to make stitches around the sides and bottom. Repeat to make two hip pockets in the back. Flatten a ⁷/₁₆" stone-look green ball to ¹/₈" thick and attach to the top of the body. Push a ¹/₂" long toothpick into the center top of the body so ¹/₄" extends.

3 **Arms:** Shape two ¹¹/₁₆" stone-look green balls into tapered logs. Attach one to each shoulder. **Straps:** Roll a ³/₈" stone-look blue ball to a 2³/₄" long log. Flatten, then cut in half. Use the round end of the pin to press a ¹/₈" white ball into the bottom of each strap. Use the pin to make two holes in each button.

4 **Frog—body:** Shape a ⁹/₁₆" green ball into an egg. Press to the center of the body. Flatten a ¹/₄" light green ball to ¹/₈" and press onto the front of the body.

Eyes: Flatten two $3/16$" green balls slightly. Use the round end of the pin to press a $1/16$" white ball into the front of each eye. Insert a seed bead (see page 7) into the middle of each white ball. Attach the eyes to the body top. Bring the boy's arms upward to wrap around the sides of the frog. **Legs:** Roll a $1/4$" green ball to 1", cut in half and attach below the frog's body, bending as shown.

5 **Hands & frog arms:** Attach a $7/16$" peach ball to the end of each arm. Shape two $3/16$" green balls into triangles. Attach one to each side of the body, over the boy's hands. Attach a $1/16$" light green ball to each arm, leg and eye for warts. **Head:** Press the center of a 1" peach ball onto the toothpick at the top of the body. Attach a $1/8$" peach ball to each side of the head for ears and use the round end of the pin to indent. Use the round end of the pin to indent three freckles in front of each ear. Insert the seed beads for eyes. **Hair:** Flatten an $11/16$" light brown ball to $1/8$" thick. Attach to the head, starting at the back and wrapping to the front. Shape two $1/4$" light brown balls into triangles. Attach, points together, in the center of the forehead for bangs. **Patches:** Flatten two $1/8$" stone-look blue balls to $1/16$". Cut each into a $1/4$" square. Attach one to each elbow and use the pin to indent two or three stitches around each.

6 **Cap:** Shape a $9/16$" white ball into a dome and attach to the top of the head. Flatten a $1/4$" stone-look blue ball to $1/16$" thick and shape into a triangle. Press onto the cap side. Flatten a $3/8$" light blue ball into a $1/8$" thick half circle. Press onto the cap side, below the triangle for a brim. Flatten a $1/8$" light blue ball and press to the top of the cap, touching the tip of the triangle. **Snake:** Roll a $5/16$" yellow ball and a $3/8$" green ball into 3" long logs. Flatten slightly, then press the green log on top of the yellow log. Roll to smooth, then coil next to the boy's shoe as shown. Use the pin to indent eyes.

7 **Dog:** Press two $3/8$" light brown balls together. Shape two $7/16$" light brown balls into tapered logs, then attach the small ends together behind the balls. Use the pin to cut two toe lines in each foot. Shape a $7/8$" light

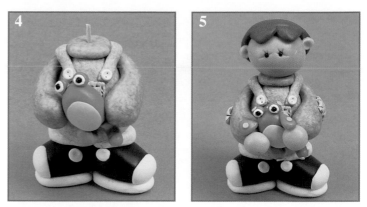

brown ball into an egg and press onto the top of the feet. Roll a $1/4$" light brown ball into a $1/2$" long tapered log. Press the wide end onto the back of the body for a tail, curving to one side as if he were wagging it.

8 **Head:** Shape a $7/8$" light brown ball into a rounded triangle. Press onto the top of the body. Insert the seed beads for eyes. **Ears:** Flatten two $3/8$" light brown balls to $1/8$" thick and shape into diamonds. Attach one to each side of the head, extending backward then forward to give the dog an alert, interested look. Shape a $3/8$" light brown ball into a rounded triangle and press onto the middle of the face for the muzzle. Attach a $1/8$" light brown ball under the muzzle. Attach a $1/8$" black ball to the muzzle center.

9 Roll a $7/16$" stone-look blue ball into a 3" long log, then flatten. Wrap it loosely around the neck and trim any excess. Attach a $1/8$" light blue ball below the collar as shown. Bake (see page 6).

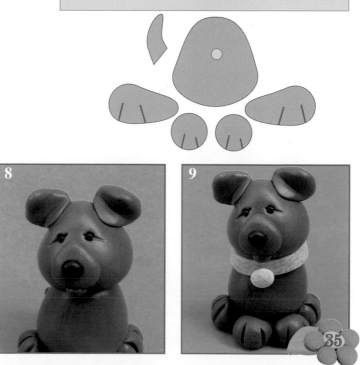

Standing Moose
by Shelly Comiskey

actual height 4⅝"

Sculpey®: raw sienna, burnt umber, ecru, yellow, green, alizarin crimson, translucent
red cotton knit child's glove
two 2½" lengths of bamboo skewer
1"x6" strip of red/green plaid fabric
clay cutters: ⅛" heart, ⅛" circle (or use these patterns) ♡ ○
chalk: brown, black, red; small paintbrush
⅝"x1" piece of beige cardstock
2" of 22-gauge black wire
1/16" hole punch
fine-tip permanent gel pens: red, green, brown, black, white
2 size 15/0 black seed beads
tacky craft glue
basic supplies (see inside the front cover)

First, blend to make:
• buckskin: 1" ball of ecru + 7/16" ball of yellow

1 **Boots**: Shape two ¾" buckskin balls into fat "L's" and flatten the top of each. Pinch out the heels. Shape two ½" translucent balls into rectangles and flatten to fit the boot bottoms. Attach one to the bottom of each boot. Use the needle to indent vertical tread lines around each sole.

2 Draw an X on the front of each boot for laces; use the stylus to poke a hole at the end of each line. Use the needle to draw stitches around the base of each boot and two rows down each boot front on each side of the laces. Roll two 5/16" sienna balls into 1" long logs and flatten. Press one around the top back of each boot, leaving a gap in front. Glue a skewer length ½" into each boot top. Press the boots together so they form a right angle. Use brown chalk to shade the boots. Bake (page 6); let cool.

3 **Body**: Shape a 1¼" crimson ball into a pear. Flatten two ½" crimson balls to ⅛" thick and press side by side onto the bottom of the body for the shorts cuffs. Apply glue to the top of each leg and set the body on them, centering a cuff over each. Press the body down until only 1" of skewer shows. Be sure the body is balanced.

4 **Arms**: Roll two ⅝" sienna balls into tapered logs. Press the wide ends flat and bend at the elbows. Attach one to each side of the body with the small ends near the top of the pear. Flatten two ⅜" burnt umber balls to ¼" thick, then pinch one side of each flatter to form a wedge. Attach one to the end of each arm. Use the stylus to indent hoof lines. Bend his left arm upward so it will be able to hold the sign. Flatten a ⅜" sienna ball onto the neck. Insert a toothpick into the neck so ¾" extends.

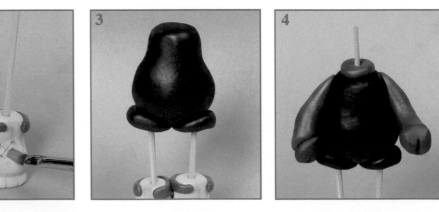

5 Use the needle to draw a line down the center front body. Draw short, random stitch marks across it. Flatten green to ¹⁄₁₆" thick. Use the heart cutter to cut four buttons and the circle cutter to cut two buttons. Use the needle to poke two holes in each. Place two hearts on the center line, angling them slightly in different directions. Flatten crimson clay to ¹⁄₁₆" thick and cut four ¼" squares. Place two on the lower front for pockets. Use the pin to draw a dashed stitching line around each pocket.

6 Use the pin to draw a stitching line down the center back as for the front. Place the remaining pockets on the bottom back and draw stitching lines around

them. Attach a heart button to the left pocket. Set the remaining buttons aside for step 9.

7 **Head**: Roll a 1" sienna ball into a pear. Angle it backward and bend the small end upward. Press the center onto the neck so the wide end extends forward. Use the stylus to poke two nostrils in the front. Insert the seed beads for eyes. Use the pin to draw a short, angled eyebrow above each eye.

8 **Ears**: Roll two ³⁄₈" sienna balls into teardrops for ears. Use the side of the stylus to indent each, then press one onto each side of the head, points upward.

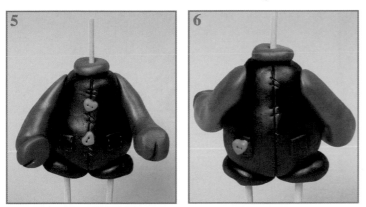

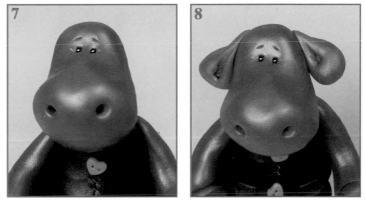

9 **Antlers**: Roll two ⅝" ecru balls into tapered logs and flatten to ¼" thick. Use the side of the pin to indent 2–3 times on one side of each; draw stitching lines around the fronts. Attach the small ends above the ears and curve upward as shown.

10 Use black chalk to shade the ears, eyes and nostrils. Use brown chalk to shade the antlers. Use red chalk to blush the cheeks. Bake (see page 6) the moose and the buttons; let cool. Seal (see page 7). **Cap**: Cut off ¾ of one glove finger. Fold the bottom to the inside as high as possible, then fold the edge up ¼". Glue between the antlers. Glue the heart button to the right brim. **Socks**: Cut two ¼"x1" strips from the remaining glove. Wrap one around each ankle, fold the end under and glue. Glue a round button to the outside of each sock.

11 **Scarf**: Fold the fabric lengthwise and tie around his neck, pulling the ends to the left.

12 **Sign**: Trace and cut out the oval pattern. Lay on the cardstock and trace with the black pen. Cut just outside the black line. Draw a black dashed line and a red line inside the black line. Write "Moose Collector" in black ink in the center. Draw a green tree with a brown trunk on each side; draw a red heart at the bottom. Outline the trees and heart in black. Use the white pen to make clusters of three dots throughout. Punch two holes ½" apart at the top. Bend the wire into a curve and insert the ends through the holes. Bend them up in back. Hang the sign on the moose's hand as shown in the large photo on page 36.

Pot of Friends
by Shohreh Dolkhani

actual height 4³/₄"

Sculpey®: pink, hot pink, green, ivory,
   pale peach, brown, black, yellow
2" wide terra cotta pot
floral moss
aluminum foil
9" of ¹/₈" wide blue satin ribbon
9" of ¹/₈" wide pink satin ribbon
9" of ¹/₈" wide yellow satin ribbon
broad-tip black permanent pen
acrylic paints: light blue, black, white
#0 liner paintbrush
pink powder blush, small paintbrush
basic supplies (see inside the front cover)

bunny
ear

1 Place three 1" balls of scrap clay (any color) into the pot. **Bunny:** Shape a ⁷/₈" ivory ball into an egg. Push a ¹/₂" length of toothpick into the top, leaving ¹/₄" exposed; repeat on the bottom. *Arms:* Shape two ¹/₂" ivory balls into tapered logs. Flatten the large ends; press the small ends onto the body.

2 *Head:* Shape a ¹¹/₁₆" ivory ball into an egg. Press onto the top toothpick. Blush the cheeks. *Nose:* Shape a ³/₁₆" pink ball into a rounded triangle. Press onto the lower face. Use the pin point to make three whisker dots on each side of the nose and to draw a vertical muzzle line under the nose.

3 *Ears:* Shape two ⁵/₈" ivory balls to match the pattern. Blush the inner ears. Pinch the bottoms and attach one to each side of the head. Tip the ends forward as shown.

4 Push the lower toothpick into the left front ball of scrap clay. Bend the arms over the side of the pot. Blush the tops of the paws.

1

2

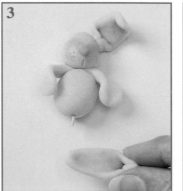

3

4

38

5 **Pig:** Follow step 1, but use peach clay.
Head: Shape a 3/4" peach ball into an egg. Press onto the top of the body. Blush the cheeks.

6 **Ears:** Flatten two 7/16" peach balls to match the pattern. Blush the inner ears. Pinch the top and bottom of each ear, use a pin to indent the center bottom as shown, then press one onto each side of the head.

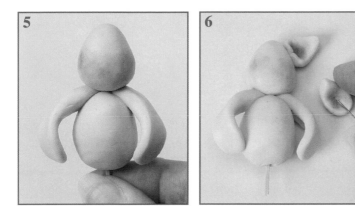

pig ear

7 **Snout:** Shape a 3/8" peach ball into an oval and flatten to 3/32" thick. Press onto the lower front of the head. Use the rounded end of the pin to imprint nostrils.

8 Push the lower toothpick into the right front ball of scrap clay. Bend the arms over the front of the pot. Use the pin point to draw a hoof line on the end of the hooves.

9 **Bear:** Shape a 1" brown ball into an egg; follow step 1 to insert toothpicks. *Arms:* Shape two 1/2" brown balls into tapered logs. Press one onto each side of the body. *Head:* Shape a 3/4" brown ball into a rounded triangle and attach to the body top.

10 *Ears:* Flatten two 1/4" brown balls to 1/8" thick. Flatten a 3/16" ivory ball onto the center of each brown ball. Press one onto each side of the head. *Muzzle:* Shape a 3/8" ivory ball into an oval and flatten to 3/32" thick. Press onto the lower half of the head. *Nose:* Shape a 3/16" black ball into a rounded triangle. Press onto the top of the muzzle. Use the pin to draw a vertical line under the nose and to make three whisker dots on each side. Blush the cheeks.

11 Push the lower toothpick into the back ball of scrap clay. Fill the pot with foil balls to adjust the characters to the placements and heights shown. Lift the bear's arms slightly and place one on the outer shoulder of each friend. **Flower & leaves:** Follow page 63 to make a hot pink flower and two leaves. Press onto the lower pot as shown in the large photo on page 38. Bake (see page 6). Paint eyes (page 7) on each friend and seal.

12 Use the broad-tip pen to write "If Friends Were Flowers, I'd Pick You" on the front of the pot as shown in the large photo. Make black dip dots on the ends of the letters. Glue the moss between the characters to cover the foil and scrap clay. Tie each ribbon length into a shoestring bow with 1/2" loops and 1/2" tails. Glue as shown in the large photo.

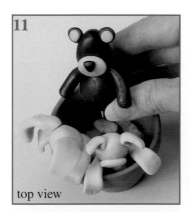
top view

top view

39

Honey Bees by Shelly Comiskey

Sculpey®: yellow, golden brown, black
2 black glass seed beads
6" length of 24-gauge wire
48" of 3-ply jute
paper, scissors
basic supplies
  (see inside the
    front cover)

actual height 2¹/₄"

1 Body: Shape a 1¹/₄" brown ball into a pear. Use the pin to draw stitches down the front of the body. **Legs:** Shape two ³/₄" brown balls into tapered logs. Indent the wide end of each with your thumb, pushing to turn up the toes. Attach the small ends to the body as shown, placing the feet 1" apart and turning the toes outward. Cut two toe lines in the top of each foot. **Arms:** Roll two ¹¹/₁₆" brown balls into tapered logs. Attach one on each side of the body, with the small ends at the shoulders, extending as shown. Cut two toe lines in the end of each arm. Use the pin to draw stitches down the tops of the arms. Attach a ¹/₈" brown ball to the lower center of the back for the tail.

2 Head: Shape a ⁷/₈" brown ball into a rounded tri-angle. Press onto the top of the body, over the arms. Roll two ³/₈" brown balls into ⁵/₈" long logs. Fold in half and pinch the ends together. Press one onto each side of the head for ears. Use the pin to draw stitches down the center of the lower face, over the head and down the back. **Muzzle:** Flatten a ³/₈" brown ball into a rounded triangle and press onto the face center. Attach a ¹/₈" black ball for the nose. Insert the seed beads (see page 7) for eyes, then use the pin to draw eyelashes and eyebrows.

3 Bow: Shape two ³/₈" yellow balls into triangles. Press the points together and attach a ¹/₈" yellow ball to the center. Use the pin to indent fold lines. Attach to the top back of the head. **Buttons:** Use the rounded end of a pin to press two ¹/₈" yellow balls into the front of the bear. Use the pin point to add two holes in each button. **Patches:** Flatten a ¹/₄" yellow ball to ¹/₁₆" thick and cut into two ¹/₄" squares. Press onto each elbow. Use the pin to make two or three indents around the edges of the patches. **Paw pads:** Flatten six ¹/₁₆" yellow balls. Press one onto the bottom of each toe. Flatten two ¹/₈" yellow balls into triangles. Press one onto each foot below the toe pads.

4 Hive: Shape a 1" scrap clay ball into a hive. Poke a hole ¹/₄" up from the bottom front. **Bees:** Press three ³/₁₆" yellow and two ³/₁₆" black balls together, alternating colors, then roll smooth. Repeat for two more bees. Press one onto the top of her right foot. Insert the wire into one bee. Push the other wire end into the back of her left arm. Remove the wire and coil around a toothpick to create a spring; set aside. Bake (see page 6). Cover the hive with glue, then wind the string around it; start at the bottom and work upward, cutting the string at the hole and starting again on the other side. Glue the hive between her legs. Glue one end of the wire into the bee and the other into the arm. Glue the last bee to the hive. Cut three sets of wings from paper and glue one set to each bee.

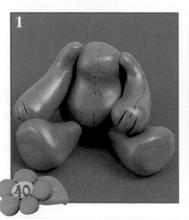

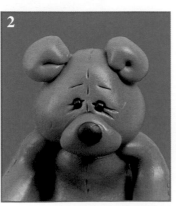

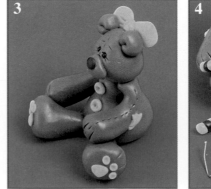

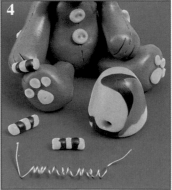

Antique Bear
by Linda Welsh

bear sits 2¹/₄" tall.

Sculpey®: pale peach, black
9" length of ¹/₂" wide burgundy & tan print
  fabric
⁵/₁₆" heart clay cutter
2 black seed beads
dark brown acrylic paint
pink chalk
small paintbrush
soft cloth
28-gauge wire
basic supplies (see inside the front cover)

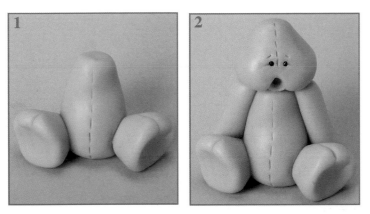

1 Body: Shape a 1" peach ball into a cone; use your fingers to round the front to plump his tummy. Use the pin to make stitch lines down his tummy. **Legs:** Shape two ¹¹/₁₆" peach balls into ⁵/₈" long tapered logs; square the tips and use your thumb to indent the soles of each foot. Press to his body to extend as shown. Use the pin to indent toe lines.

2 Arms: Shape two ¹¹/₁₆" peach balls into 1³/₈" long tapered logs. Use the pin to make stitch lines along the outside of each. Press the narrow ends to his shoulders. **Head:** Shape a ⁷/₈" peach ball into a rounded triangle. Use the pin to make stitch lines down the front. Use the knife to cut a ¹/₂" slit in the bottom center. Use your fingers to round each muzzle bottom. Roll and insert a ³/₁₆" peach ball for a mouth and close the slit slightly. Use the paintbrush handle to indent a hole in the mouth. Press a seed bead on each side of the stitches for eyes; use the pin to make lashes and brows. Insert a toothpick into his neck leaving ¹/₂" exposed and press his head onto it.

3 Muzzle and ears: Roll a ¹/₄" peach ball into a ³/₈" long oval, flatten one side and press the flattened side to his face beneath his eyes. Roll a ¹/₈" black ball and press for his nose. Roll two ⁷/₁₆" peach balls and flatten slightly. Press to each side of his head for ears. Use the paintbrush handle to indent ¹/₈" wide holes as shown. Use the pin to make stitch likes along the outside of each ear.

4 Use the heart cutter to imprint a heart in each foot bottom. Use the pin to make stitch lines around each heart. Use the paintbrush and chalk to color each heart and to blush each cheek. Bake (see page 6) then antique (see page 7). Use the fabric to make a collar bow and glue it to his right shoulder.

41

Friends Forever
by Shelly Comiskey

Sculpey®: white, orange, yellow, black, tan, pale peach, stone-look pink, stone-look purple,
4 black glass seed beads
pink chalk
small flat paintbrush
basic supplies (see inside the front cover)
optional: ½" heart clay cutter

actual height 2½"

1 **Blond girl:** Roll two ³/₄" peach balls into 1" long tapered logs. Attach to a ³/₄" white ball, angled so the ankles are 1" apart. Flatten a ½" white ball on the end of each leg for socks.

2 **Shoes:** Shape two ³/₄" black balls into ovals and slightly flatten one end of each. Attach to the socks, extending upward. Flatten a ³/₈" black ball to ¹/₁₆" thick. Slice two ⁵/₈"x¹/₈" pieces. Wrap one around the top of each shoe and across the sock front, letting some white show through. Use the round end of the pin to press a ¹/₈" white ball to the outside of each strap.

3 **Dress:** Shape a 1¹/₈" pink ball into a cone. Use your thumb to hollow the bottom and flare the hem until you can fit it over the base so it extends to the floor in back and forward to cover her legs as shown. **Arms:** Roll two ¹¹/₁₆" white balls into 1¹/₄" long tapered logs. Attach the small end of one to each shoulder. Attach one ³/₈" peach ball to the end of each arm. Bend the arms upward to rest on the legs.

4 **Straps:** Roll a ³/₈" pink ball into a 1¹/₂" long log and flatten slightly. Cut in half and wrap one half over each shoulder, with the ends meeting in the back. Use the round end of the pin to press a ¹/₈" white ball into the bottom of each strap. Use the pin point to make two holes in each button. Push a ¹/₂" length of toothpick into the top of the body, leaving ¹/₄" exposed. **Head:** Slightly flatten a 1" peach ball. Press the center onto the toothpick.

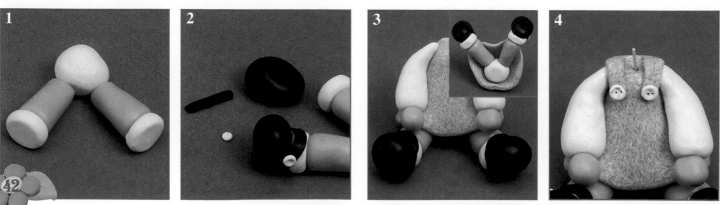

5 **Face:** Insert two seed beads (see page 7) for eyes and use the pin to draw eyelashes and eyebrows. Rub the paintbrush on the chalk, then use it to blush the cheeks. **Heart:** Flatten a $3/8$" purple ball to $1/8$" thick and shape to match the heart pattern (or use the clay cutter). Attach to the dress front. Use the pin to make stitches around the edge.

6 **Hair:** Mix a $7/8$" white ball with a $7/16$" yellow ball. Flatten a $3/4$" ball of this into a $1 1/8$"x$1 5/8$" oval. Attach to her head, starting at the bottom back and wrapping to the front. Shape two $1/4$" blond balls into triangles. Attach the points in the center of the forehead. Use the pin to indent hair lines. Flatten two $1/4$" pink balls to $1/8$" thick and attach one to each side of the head. Use the rounded end of the pin to make a hole in the center of each. Shape two $3/8$" blond balls cones and flatten slightly. Insert the points into the pink holes.

7 **Auburn-haired girl:** Repeat steps 1–5, replacing pink clay with purple clay. Make the heart out of pink clay. Make three pin pricks on each cheek for freckles. **Hair:** Mix a $1/2$" tan ball with a $3/4$" orange ball to make auburn. Shape a $3/4$" ball of this into a $3/16$" thick half circle. Attach it to her head, with the straight edge at the bottom back of the head and wrapping to the front.

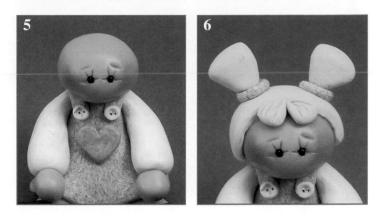

8 **Bangs:** Shape two $1/4$" auburn balls into triangles. Press the points together and attach in the center of the forehead for bangs. Use the pin to indent hair lines. Roll a $1/4$" purple ball to $7/8$" long. Flatten, then attach just behind her bangs. Shape two $1/4$" purple balls into triangles. Press the points together and attach a $3/16$" purple ball to the center. Use the pin to indent fold lines. Attach to the top of the headband. Insert a $1/2$" long toothpick into the lower right side of the blond girl. Press the auburn girl onto the toothpick, attaching the lower bodies and arms. Bake (see page 6), then seal (see page 7).

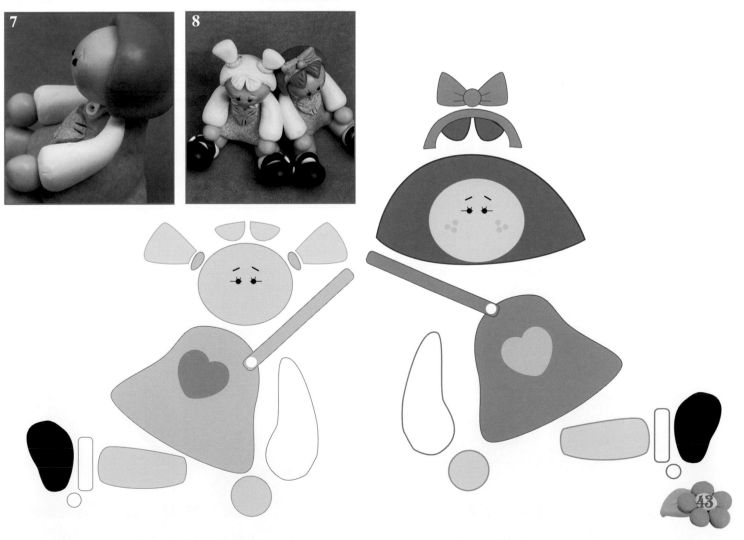

43

Old MacDonald
by Shohreh Dolkhani

Sculpey®: yellow, orange, red, pale peach, white, stone-look blue, tan, black, brown, ivory
$5^1/2$"x$2^1/2$"x$1^1/2$" wood block
$1/4$" square stencil
floral moss
garlic press or Kemper Klaygun
$1/2$" tall copper cowbell
acrylic paints: light blue, black, white
paintbrushes: #0 liner, #2 round
stiff toothbrush
broad-tip black permanent pen
basic supplies (see inside the front cover)

actual width $5^1/2$"

1 Shoes: Shape two $7/16$" ivory balls into eggs and flatten them to $1/8$". Use the pin to indent the sides every $1/8$" to create the look of tread. Shape two $5/8$" brown balls into eggs. Press them onto the soles.

2 Legs: Shape two $9/16$" stone-look blue balls into 1" long tapered logs. Press the wide end of each onto the back of a shoe. **Pant cuffs:** Mix a $1/2$" stone-look blue ball with a $5/16$" white ball. Roll the clay into a $1/4$"x5" log, then flatten to $1/16$" thick. Cut in half. Wrap one half around each leg just above the shoe; cut off excess. Push a $1/2$" length of toothpick into each leg, leaving $1/4$" exposed. Place the legs side by side.

3 Body: Shape a 1" stone-look blue ball into an egg. Flatten slightly and press onto the legs. Push a $1/2$" length of toothpick into the top front, leaving $1/4$" exposed. **Arms:** Shape two $9/16$" orange balls into tapered logs. Press one onto each side of the body. Press a $3/8$" peach ball onto the end of each arm.

4 Straps: Roll two $1/8$"x$1^1/2$" stone-look blue logs. Flatten to $1/16$" thick. Wrap over the shoulders, crossing them in back. **Pocket:** Flatten a $1/4$" tan ball to $1/16$" and shape into a rectangle. Press onto the front below the straps. Use the pin to draw stitches around the inside. **Buttons:** Use the pin head to press a $1/8$" black ball onto the end of each strap. Use the pin to make two holes in the center of each button.

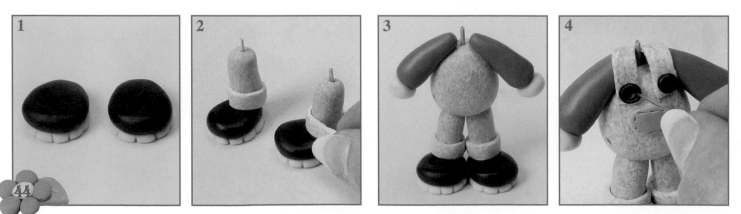

5 Follow pages 68–69, steps 4–6 to make his head, beard, mustache, nose, ears and brows. **Hair:** Roll a $1/4$"x$1$1/4" white log. Curve and flatten to $1$3/4" long. Wrap around the head back.

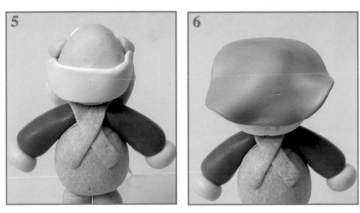

hair

6 **Hat:** Flatten an $11/16$" tan ball into a $1$3/4"x1" oval and drape over the head as shown. Press an $11/16$" tan ball onto a flat surface to flatten one side. Mold into a squarish shape and attach to the brim center as shown in the large photo on page 44. Fold up the brim in front. Use the pin to draw a # on the right side.

hat brim

7 **Cow:** Shape four $5/6$"x1" long white tapered logs. Press them together. Push a $1/2$" length of toothpick into each leg, leaving $1/4$" exposed. Shape a 1" white ball into an egg. Press onto the legs. Push a $1/2$" length of toothpick into the top front, leaving $1/4$" exposed. *Head:* Shape an $11/16$" white ball into an egg. Press onto the body.

8 *Muzzle:* Flatten a $3/8$" peach ball to $3/32$" thick and shape to match the pattern. Press onto the lower head. Use a toothpick to indent nostrils. *Ears:* Shape two $5/16$" white balls into teardrops. Press one onto each side of the head. Blush the ears.

muzzle

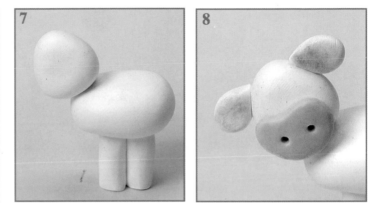

9 *Tail:* Shape a $1/8$"x1" white log and flatten one end. Press onto the rump and curl as shown. *Hair:* Press black clay through a garlic press to $1/4$"–$1/2$" long; cut off. Press some onto the top of the head for bangs. Press the rest onto the end of the tail. *Horns:* Shape a $1/8$"x$3/4$" ivory log, tapering both ends. Attach between the ears and bend the ends upward. Push the wire hook of the cow bell into the clay under the muzzle. **Pig:** Follow steps 1–3 on page 67 to make the pig.

10 **Chick:** Shape a $5/8$" yellow ball into an egg. Shape two $5/16$" yellow balls into teardrops and press one onto each side of the body. Roll a $1/8$"x$1/4$" red log. Press onto the top of the head. Use the pin to imprint comb lines. Shape a $1/8$" orange ball into a cone and attach for a beak.

11 **Flower:** Follow page 63 to make a white flower. Use the pin to make many dots on the yellow center and 1–2 lines down the center of each petal. Bake (see page 6) each piece.

12 Paint eyes (see page 7) on each character. Mix two parts water with three parts black paint. Use this mixture to paint spots randomly on the cow. **Base:** Paint the wood block blue. Let dry. Stencil two rows of white checks across each end of one $5$1/4"x$1$1/2" side. Stencil one row of checks along the top and the bottom. Spatter the front with white, then with black paint. Use the fine-tip pen to draw a — ‖ border around the front. Use the broad-tip pen to write "EIEIO" inside the border. Make black dip dots on the ends of the letters. Glue MacDonald, the cow and the pig to the top of the base. Cover the exposed block with moss. Glue the chicken and flower into the moss.

top view

45

Claudette Cow
by Judy Ferrill

Sculpey®: white, red, turquoise, flesh pink,
 green, yellow, black
one 1³/8" wide straw hat
clay cutters: ¹/4" flower, ³/16" heart (or use the
 patterns) ♥ ✿
acrylic paint: black, white; #0 liner brush
pink powder blush, small paintbrush
#3 wide white perle cotton or heavy white
 carpet thread
four ¹/4" wide white buttons with 2 holes
basic supplies (see inside the front cover)

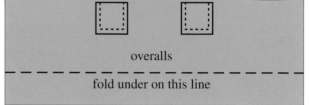

overalls

fold under on this line

First, blend to make:
• gray: 1 package of black + ¹/2 package of white

1 **Body:** Roll a 1¹/2" red ball into a 1⁵/8" tall cone. Trace and cut out the overalls pattern. Flatten turquoise clay to ¹/16" thick, lay the pattern on it and cut around it. Mark the pocket positions. Wrap the overalls around her body with the fold line even with the body bottom. Join the back edges and smooth the seam. Fold the excess under and smooth. Use your finger to indent the bottom front. Cut out the pockets and attach; use a toothpick tip to draw stitching lines around the pockets. Cut two ¹/8"x1¹/2" strips of flattened turquoise and attach for suspenders. Flatten red clay to ¹/16" thick and cut four hearts. Attach for buttons, front and back. Use the toothpick to make button holes.

2 **Head:** Roll a ³/4" white ball and follow the general directions to attach it to the body. Flatten a ³/8" ball of flesh pink into a ⁵/8" long oval and attach for the muzzle. Use a toothpick to indent a mouth and nostrils. Blush the muzzle. Roll two ¹/4" white balls and attach for ears. Press the hat onto the head as shown. **Tail:** Roll a ¹/8"x1" white rope and attach to the body back, curling it to one side. Score hair lines in the end.

3 **Legs:** Roll two ³/8"x1¹/4" red logs; repeat with turquoise. Roll four ¹/2" white balls and press one onto the bottom of each leg. Roll the legs to smooth the balls and flatten the sides. Roll four ³/8" gray balls and flatten one to fit the bottom of each leg. Indent with a knife to form cloven hooves. From the flattened turquoise, cut two ¹/4"x1¹/4" strips and wrap one around each blue leg for a cuff. Imprint stitches around the cuff tops as for the pockets.

4 **Flowers:** Roll a ¹/16"x3" green rope and cut into three 1" long stems. Drape the stems over her right "hand." Flatten yellow clay to ¹/16" thick and cut three flowers. Roll three ¹/16" red balls and press one into the center of each flower. Attach the flowers in a cluster over the stems, bending the petals upward as shown. Pierce, bake and finish the cow (see page inside the back cover). Paint black spots on her face and hooves as shown in the large photo. Assemble.

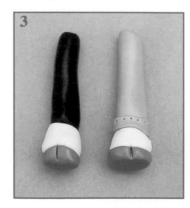

Helen Hen & her Chick

by Judy Ferrill

Sculpey®: white, gold, green, yellow, red, pink, purple,
*   sea green*
one 3/4" wide wicker basket
acrylic paint: black, white; #0 liner paintbrush
pink powder blush, small paintbrush
#3 wide white perle cotton or heavy white
*   carpet thread*
four 1/4" wide white buttons with 2 holes
3" length of 24-gauge copper wire, wire cutters
1/4" wide plastic drinking straw
basic supplies (see inside the front cover)

1 Body: Shape a 1 1/8" white ball into a 1 1/2" tall cone; pinch out a tail at the bottom back. Roll a 7/8" ball for the head and attach following the general directions. Pinch a 3/8" yellow ball into a cone and attach for her beak. Use a toothpick to draw nostrils and a mouth line. Flatten two 3/16" red balls into flattened teardrops and attach under the beak for wattles.

2 Hat: Flatten a 5/8" green ball to 1 1/2" across. Place it on her head, flaring the edges to form a brim. Roll two 1/8"x2" green ropes. Attach one to each side of the brim and loop them in a bow under her chin. Flatten three 1/8" green balls into leaves and attach in a triangle at the left side of the brim. Roll three 1/6"x1/2" pink ropes, flatten each and fold into a coil for flower buds. Attach in a cluster over the leaves. Roll five 1/16" purple balls and attach among the flowers.

3 Wings: Flatten and shape two 3/4" white balls to match the pattern, indenting the edges with a knife. Use the straw to imprint half-circle feather lines. **Legs:** Shape two 5/8" white balls into rounded cones, matching the leg top pattern. Imprint as for the wings. Shape two 1/4"x1 1/4" gold logs, flatten one end of each and notch to form toes. Turn the toes up. Use the knife to imprint horizontal lines. Attach one to the flat end of each leg top.

4 Chick: Roll a 7/16" yellow ball for the body; attach a 3/8" yellow ball for the head. Pinch a 1/8" gold ball into a cone for the beak; imprint a mouth and nostrils on the beak and two holes for eyes. Flatten two 3/16" yellow balls into teardrops and attach for wings. Press the chick to the lower left side of the hen's body. **Eggs:** Roll a 1/4" white ball into an oval and place in the basket. Repeat until the basket is filled. **Glasses:** Wrap the center of the wire around a paintbrush handle to form a circle; repeat 1/8" away. Bend the ends back and trim to 1/2" long. Attach as shown in the large photo. Pierce, bake, finish and assemble (see inside the back cover).

leaf

wing

glasses

body (side view)

tail

leg top

chick wing

foot

47

actual height 1⅝"

Spring Hen & Chick
by Anita Behnen

Sculpey®: white, cadmium yellow, red pearl, translucent
2 yellow vinyl-coated paper clips, wire cutters
2½" square of black sunflower-print fabriclay (see inside the back cover)
⅛ tsp. of black embossing powder
red chalk, small paintbrush
black seed beads: 2 size 12/0, 2 size 15/0
three ½" long strands of white thread
one 1" long white fluffy feather
³⁄₁₆" heart clay cutter (or use the pattern) ♥
basic supplies (see inside the front cover)

First, knead the embossing powder into a 2" ball of white clay. In the following instructions, "white" refers to this blend.

1 **Hen:** Shape a ¾" white ball into an egg. Use the wire cutters to cut off the curved ends of the paper clips, leaving 1" long straight wire pieces. Insert one into the body top so ¼" extends. Insert two ⅝" apart into the bottom body base, angled outward, so ¾" extends.

2 **Shoes:** Shape two ½" yellow balls into ovals. Flatten slightly, pressing the backs thinner. **Socks:** Shape two ⅜" red balls into cones. Press a red cone firmly onto each shoe back. Flatten two ³⁄₁₆" balls of red clay to ¹⁄₁₆" thick and press one onto the top of each sock. Use the pin to imprint ribbing lines.

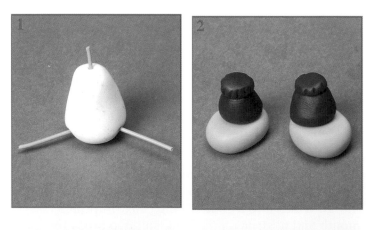

3 Roll a ¼" yellow ball into a ¹⁄₁₆" thick snake. Cut in half and wrap a strip over the base of each sock as shown, attaching the ends to the shoes. Cut off any excess. Press a ¹⁄₁₆" yellow ball onto the outer end of each strap; use the pin to poke two holes in each. Press the feet onto the lower wires so that ¼" of the clip remains visible.

4 **Dress:** Cut a 2" circle of fabriclay (see page 7). Cut a slit from one side to the center, then wrap it around the body, overlapping the cut edges in the back. Glue to secure.

back view

5 **Wings:** Roll two ½" white balls into 1" long logs. Flatten each end to form elongated diamonds. Bend at the elbows. Apply glue to the inside tops and press them against the shoulders of the dress.

6 **Head:** Shape a 9/16" white ball into an egg. Insert the 12/0 seed beads for eyes, adding an extra smile line at the outer corner of each eye. Shape a 3/16" yellow ball into a cone and attach to the lower face. Use the pin to draw a smile and poke nostrils. Firmly press the head onto the neck wire. Blush the cheeks using the chalk and small paintbrush.

7 **Hat:** Shape a ¾" red ball into a cone. Push your finger into the base, then use the fingers of your other hand to flatten the top flat and pinch a brim all around—the hat is 1" wide and ½" tall. Cut a ⅛"x2½" strip of fabriclay and wrap around the base of the crown. Place the hat firmly on her head and fold the front brim up as shown.

8 **Flower:** Shape five ⅛" pure white balls (no embossing powder) into teardrops and flatten each. Arrange in a circle, points together, on the turned-up hat brim. Press a 1/16" yellow ball into the flower center.

9 **Chick:** Shape a ⅝" white ball into an egg. *Boots:* Shape two ⅜" yellow balls into tapered logs and bend each into an L. Pinch the heels to a point and round the toes. Attach to the bottom of the egg extending outward as shown.

10 **Beak:** Shape a ⅛" yellow ball into a cone and attach ⅓ of the way down the body. Use the pin to draw a smile and to poke two nostril holes in the beak top. Insert the 15/0 seed beads above the beak. Blush the cheeks.

11 **Wings:** Pinch two ¼" white balls into elongated diamonds about ½" long. Bend at the elbows and attach one to each side, placing the tops even with the bottom of the beak. Push the wing tips forward so they touch.

12 **Heart:** Flatten red clay to 1/16" thick and cut a heart. Attach to the chest above the wing tips. Use the pin to poke a hole in the top of the head and deepen the indent in the heart.

(Refer to the large photo on page 48.) Press the chick against the hen's dress with its back against her leg. Wrap her wing around the chick. Bake (see page 6); let cool, then seal. Glue the feather to the hat brim behind the flower. Glue the threads into the hole of the chick's head. Once the glue has dried, cut the threads to ⅛" long.

Summer Rooster
by Anita Behnen

*Sculpey®: white, cadmium yellow, red
  pearl, translucent*
1/8 tsp. of black embossing powder
2 yellow vinyl-coated paper clips
wire cutters
*2" square of black sunflower-print
  fabriclay (see inside the back cover)*
red chalk, small paintbrush
3/4" tall metal watering can
2 size 12/0 black seed beads
one 2 1/2" long white fluffy feather
6–8 assorted dried miniflowers
basic supplies (see inside the front cover)

First, knead the embossing powder into a
1 3/4" ball of white clay. In the following
instructions, "white" refers to this blend.

actual height 1 3/4"

1 **Body**: Follow page 48, step 1, but use a 7/8" white
ball. **Boots**: Roll two 9/16" yellow balls into 1" long
tapered logs. Bend each in half; pinch the bend to form
the heel, then round the toe. Use the pin to score around
each boot side just above the bottom to separate the
sole. Press the side of the pin across the sole to create
a heel. Poke three pairs of holes up the front and draw
a line between them as shown. Flatten two 1/4" white
balls and press one onto the top of each boot. Use the
pin to draw vertical ribbing lines. Press the boots onto
the lower wires so that 1/4" of the clip remains visible.

2 **Vest**: Trace and cut out the pattern. Place on the
clay side of the fabriclay and trace around it with
the pin. Cut out. Wrap the vest around his body with
the opening in the front.

3 **Wings and head**: Follow page 49, steps 5–6, but
use a 5/8" ball. Blush the cheeks. Roll three 1/8" red
balls into cones and attach to the top of his head in a
row, points up. Press the watering can into the angle of
his legs. Apply glue to the inner wing tips and press
them onto the can as shown.

4 Use the pin to poke a hole in his back below the
vest for the feather, angling it downward so the
feather will extend up for a tail. Place the feather in
the hole to be sure it will fit, then remove it. Bake the
rooster (see page 6) and let cool, then seal (see page 7).
Glue the feather into the hole. Glue the dried flowers
into the watering can as shown in the large photo.

vest

back view

She sits 3" tall.

An Apple for Teacher
by Linda Welsh

*Sculpey®: brown, red opalescent, blue, pale peach,
    white, green, black*
clay cutters: 3/16" and 1/2" hearts, 3/8" teardrop
4" length of 24-gauge gold wire, needle-nose pliers
white acrylic paint, two black seed beads
pink powder blush
basic supplies (see inside the front cover)

1 Shoes: Flatten two 5/8" black balls to 3/8" thick
ovals. **Socks:** Flatten two 1/4" white balls; shape
over each shoe top center. Flatten two 7/16" white balls
and press over the heel for sock rolls. Wrap a 1/8"x1"
black log across each ankle for a strap. **Legs:** Shape
two 3/4" peach balls to 1 1/2" long logs; press one end to
each sock roll. Angle the toe tips toward you.

2 Dress: Shape a 1 1/2"x1 1/2" blue cone. Use a pin to
indent the bottom edge for ruffles. Press the dress
on top of the legs, feet extended 1" apart. **Arms:** Shape
1 1/4" long blue tapered logs. Indent an elbow bend in
her right arm. Press a 7/16" peach ball to each wide end.
Attach the arms to her dress as shown. Insert half a
toothpick into her right hand extending as shown.

3 Collar: Flatten white clay to 1/16" thick; cut a
1 1/8" wide circle. Make scallops (see page 7) and
use the pin to dot each. Drape the collar over her
shoulders; insert a toothpick to extend 1/2" from her
neck. Roll two 1/8" red balls, indent each with the pin
head and press to the collar. **Head:** Roll a 7/8" peach
ball and press onto the toothpick. Roll a 1/16" peach
ball, indent with the pin head and press for her left
ear. Press two seed beads for eyes. Use the pin to
poke two holes for the glasses as shown. **Glasses:** Use
the needle-nose pliers to shape the wire the pattern
above to make 1/8" wide lenses. Insert the glasses into
the holes in her face. Use the paintbrush and chalk
to blush her cheeks. **Hair:** Flatten brown clay to 1/8"
thick, cut a 1 1/8" circle and press to her head for
hair. Roll two 5/8" brown balls into 1" long tapered
logs, shape in an "S" and attach as shown. Roll three
1/8"x1/2" brown logs. Place for bangs, curve each side
bang as shown and trim the center bang to 3/8".

4 Bow: Flatten red clay to 3/16" thick and cut two
1/4"x1/2" strips and two large hearts. Indent an
inverted "V" on an end of each strip and place on her
hair. Attach the hearts, points together, press a 1/8" red
ball to the center and indent with the pin. **Book:** Use
the pattern to cut 1/16" thick brown and white clay. Fold
the white piece into the brown piece; cut and place
a small red heart and use the pin to write "ABC" as
shown. Place the book on her right toothpick. **Apple:**
Use the pattern to shape a 1" red ball. Flatten green
clay to 1/8" thick and cut two teardrops. Insert a 1/2"
long toothpick and place the leaves as shown. Use the
pin to indent each leaf, press the apple onto her left
hand and remove the stem. Bake (see page 6). Glue
and replace the apple stem. Dip the pin head into white
paint and touch it to the apple and drag the pin head in
a comma shape for a highlight. Seal.

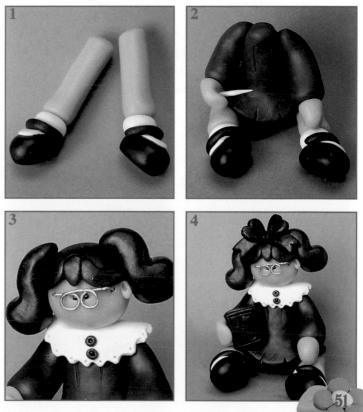

51

Lion & Lamb

by Shohreh Dolkhani

Sculpey®: dark green, bright green,
  pink, violet, purple, gray, white, tan,
  brown, black, yellow
garlic press
pink powder blush, small paintbrush
acrylic paint: light blue, black, white
#0 liner brush
fine tip black permanent marker
basic supplies (see inside the front
  cover)

actual width 3¹/₂"

base

1 **Base:** Flatten a 1¹/₈" dark green ball to match the pattern. **Lion:** Shape a 1¹/₈" tan ball into an egg. Press onto the back of the base. Push a ¹/₂" length of toothpick into the top front, leaving ¹/₄" exposed. **Head:** Shape a 1" tan ball into a rounded triangle. Press onto the toothpick. Blush the cheeks. **Muzzle:** Flatten two ¹/₄" tan balls on the lower head. Use the pin to make three dots in each ball. **Nose:** Flatten a ³/₁₆" black ball into a rounded triangle. Press onto the muzzle. **Paws:** Roll two ⁵/₁₆" tan balls into ovals and press onto the body front. Use the pin to draw toe lines. **Tail:** Roll a ¹/₈"x1¹/₄" long tan log. Press onto the rump and curl as shown.

2 **Ears:** Use the pin head to press a ¹/₄" tan ball onto each side of the head. Remove the pin, leaving an indent. **Mane:** Press brown clay through the garlic press to ¹/₄"–¹/₂" long. Cut off with the knife. Use a toothpick to pick up strands and attach to the head, curling them for a natural look. Use several strands for the tail tuft.

3 **Lamb:** Shape a ⁵/₈" gray ball into an egg. Attach in front of the lion as shown. **Head:** Shape a ⁹/₁₆" gray ball into a rounded triangle. Press the large end onto the top front body. Blush the cheeks. **Nose:** Shape a ¹/₈" pink ball into an oval and flatten. Press onto the lower face. **Ears:** Shape two ¹/₄" gray balls into teardrops. Press one onto each side of the head. **Wool:** Make as for the lion's mane, but use white clay. **Tail:** Press a ¹/₄" gray ball onto the body back. **Hooves:** Roll two ³/₁₆" gray balls into ovals and press onto the body front. Use the pin to draw toe lines.

4 **Flowers:** Place five ³/₁₆" pink balls in a circle and flatten slightly. Flatten a ³/₁₆" yellow ball onto the center. Repeat for a violet and a purple flower. **Leaves:** Flatten three ¹/₄" bright green balls and shape to match the pattern. Use the pin to draw the center line. Press the flowers and leaves onto the base as shown. Bake (see page 6). Paint the eyes (see page 7), then seal.

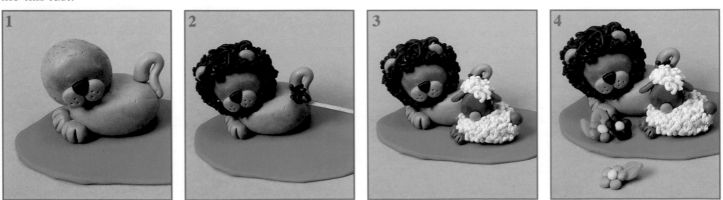

Sparkle Unicorn

by Shelly Comiskey

Sculpey®: white, fluorescent pink
hot pink acrylic paint, ¼" flat paintbrush
embossing powders: ¼ tsp. of light sparkle, ¼ tsp. of
   hot pink
white metallic yarn
2 size 15/0 black seed beads
basic supplies (see inside the front cover)

First, paint the top half of a toothpick pink; set aside to dry. Flatten a 1½" ball of white clay, pour on the embossing powders and fold the clay over. Knead until the powder is spread evenly throughout the clay. This blend is used for the entire unicorn except the horseshoes. When baked, the colors of the embossing powders intensify.

1 **Body**: Shape a 1" clay ball into a pear. **Back legs**: Shape two ¾" balls into 1" long tapered logs and flatten the wide ends. Use your thumb to push up a hoof on each. Attach to the body sides extending outward. **Front legs**: Shape two ⅝" balls into 1" long tapered logs as for the back legs. Attach to the body front inside the back legs as shown. Use the needle to draw hair lines at the top of each hoof.

2 **Horseshoes**: Roll a ⅜" pink ball into a ⅛" thick snake and cut two 1½" lengths. Curve one in a semicircle on the bottom of each back hoof and flatten slightly. Press a ⅛" pink ball on each end of each shoe and one into each center front. Pinch the center balls into a point. Poke holes around the bottom of each shoe.

3 **Head**: Shape a ⅞" ball into a rounded triangle and attach to the top of the body. Insert a 1" toothpick length into the body top and press the head onto it, tilting it slightly left. Gently flatten a ⅜" ball onto the head front. Use the stylus to indent nostrils. Insert the beads for eyes (see page 7). **Ears**: Shape two ⅛" balls into cones. Attach to the head and indent with the stylus. **Horn**: Cut the pink half off the painted toothpick and insert into the forehead. **Mane**: Pinch off several small clay pieces and roll into ⅛"–¼" long teardrops. Attach over the top of the head and down the neck, with some extending forward from between the ears. Use the needle to arrange the hair and draw hair lines. **Tail**: Roll a ½" ball into a 1" long teardrop and attach at the center back extending to the unicorn's left. Use the needle to draw hair lines.

4 Blush the cheeks. Bake; let cool—don't touch the piece while it's hot, as the embossing powder may smear. Fray out short strands of metallic yarn and glue randomly to the mane and forelock to add sparkle.

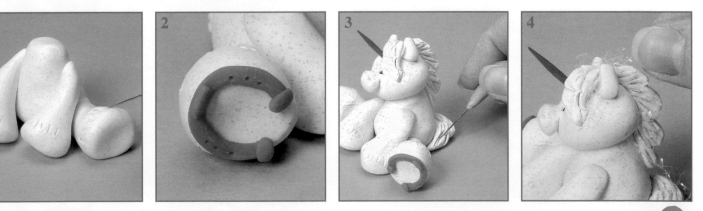

Polka-Dot Girl
by Shelly Comiskey

actual height 4" excluding hair

Sculpey®: white, black, beige, fuchsia, translucent
4" square of black flower-print fabriclay (see inside the back cover)
2 size 15/0 black seed beads
pink chalk, small paintbrush
clay cutters: 3/16" heart, 3/8" heart, 1/2" flower (or use these patterns)
2" of 28-gauge black wire
bamboo skewer, wire cutters
white acrylic paint
blonde Country Curls doll hair
basic supplies (see inside the front cover)

First, blend to make:
• dark pink: 1" ball of fuchsia + 3/4" ball of white

1 **Shoes**: Shape two 3/4" black balls into eggs and flatten slightly. Press the heel ends together with the toes angled apart. Shape two 3/8" white balls into ovals and flatten. Lay one on the top back of each shoe. Roll a 3/8" black ball into a 1 1/2" long rope, flatten and cut in half. Wrap one half over the top of each shoe as shown.

2 Attach a 3/8" white ball to the top of each shoe behind the strap. Flatten white clay to 1/16" and use the flower cutter to make two flowers. Attach one to the top of each sock; use the pin to imprint a dot in each petal. Roll two 1/8" dark pink balls and attach one to the outside of each shoe strap for a button. Cut two 2 1/2" lengths of skewer and insert one into each foot as shown, leaving 2" exposed. Bake (see page 6).

3 **Body**: Shape a 1" white ball into a pear. Apply glue to the tops of the skewer legs, then press the large end of the body down onto the legs so 1" of skewer is exposed.

4 **Dress**: Cut a 3" circle of fabriclay (see page 7). Cut a slit from one side to the center, then wrap it around the body, overlapping the cut edges in the back. Glue to secure. Pinch and ruffle the dress into graceful folds, pressing it against the body·

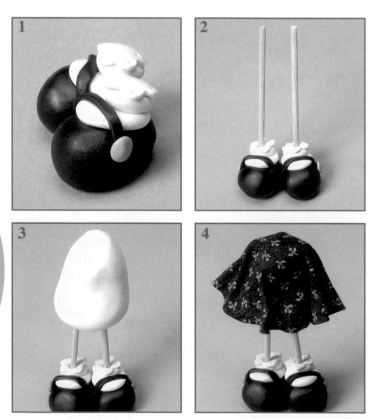

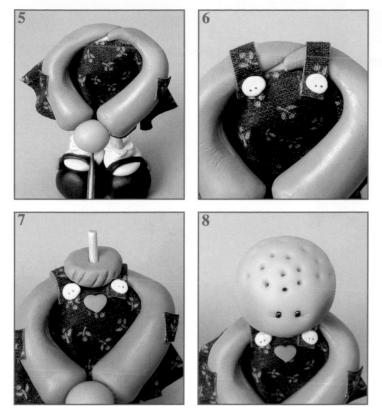

5 Arms: Roll two ½" dark pink balls into 1⅜" long tapered logs. Bend at the elbows and attach the small ends to the shoulders. Cut two ¼" squares of fabriclay and glue one onto each elbow. Press the wrists together, then attach a ⅜" beige ball for the clasped hands. Use the stylus to poke a hole in the bottom of the hands.

6 Shoulder straps: Cut two ⅛"x½" fabriclay strips. Attach one over each shoulder, securing each end with glue. Apply glue to the front end of each strap. Flatten a 1/16" white ball onto each for a button. Use the needle to poke two holes in each button.

7 Flatten dark pink clay to 1/16" and cut a 3/16" heart. Glue it to the top front of the dress. Flatten a ⅜" fuchsia ball to ⅛" thick and use the side of the needle to indent evenly spaced ribs around the outside. Attach to the top of the dress. Insert ½ of a toothpick into the top so ¼" extends.

8 Head: Roll a ⅞" beige ball and press onto the neck toothpick. Use the stylus to poke ⅛" deep holes ⅛" apart over the hair area. Insert the seed beads for the eyes. Use the pin to make an extra crease outside each eye. Blush the cheeks. Check that she can stand upright; use an X-acto® knife to trim the soles of her shoes if needed for balance.

9 Garland hearts: Flatten dark pink clay to ⅛" thick. Use the cutter to make two ⅜" hearts. Use the pin to poke a hole in the top of each heart. **Bow:** Cut the bow pattern below from fabriclay. Fold the ends to the back so they just meet and glue to secure. Press a ⅛" dark pink ball into the bow center. Use the pin to poke two holes in the ball. Bake the hearts, bow and doll; let cool.

10 Glue one end of the wire into each heart. Bend the wire in half and glue the bend into the hole in the bottom of the hands. Use the toothpick with white acrylic paint to make polka dots on the hearts and the doll's sleeves.

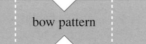

bow pattern

11 Hair: Cut the hair into 6" pieces—as many as there are holes in the head, plus one. Apply a drop of glue to a hole. Fold a hair strand in half and twist the folded end. Use the pin to press the twisted end into the hole. Repeat for the remaining holes—don't apply glue to more than three holes at a time. Once all the hair is applied, let the glue dry for 30 minutes.

12 Gather all the hair above the head, wrap with the last hair strand and knot the strand in back. Blend the ends into the rest of the hair. Trim the hair as needed. Glue the bow to the ponytail front over the wrapped area.

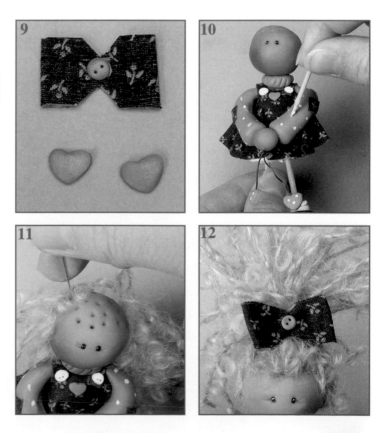

55

Rag Doll sits 2¹/₂" tall.

Garden Rag Doll
by Linda Welsh

Sculpey®: blue, gray, pale peach, yellow, tan, burgundy, green, orange
2 black seed beads
three ³/₄"x6" strips of natural muslin fabric
¹/₂"x4" strips of burgundy checked fabric
soft cloth, coffee stirrer
clay cutters: ³/₁₆" heart, ¹/₂" flower, ⁵/₁₆" teardrop
dark brown acrylic paint
pink chalk, small paintbrush
18" of 16-gauge wire
basic supplies (see inside the front cover)

leg

First, blend to make:
- slate blue (for dress): 1¹/₂" blue ball + ⁷/₈" gray ball
- light pink (for collar): ³/₈" burgundy ball + 1" peach + ³/₄" white ball
- dark pink (for patch): ⁵/₈" burgundy ball + ³/₄" white
- light green: ⁵/₈" green ball + ³/₄" white

1 **Body:** Shape a 1¹/₈" peach ball into a 1"x1¹/₄" cone. **Legs:** Shape two ¹¹/₁₆" peach balls into tapered logs indenting the tops and turning the ends up as shown on the pattern. Use the pin to draw stitches on each foot bottom and press a leg to each body side extending at a right angle, toes angled out.

2 **Dress:** Flatten the slate blue ball to ¹/₈" thick; cut a 2³/₄" circle and scallop the edges (see page 7). Use the coffee stirrer end to stamp a design in each scallop. Drape the dress over the body and legs; shape it into ruffles around the body. **Arms:** Shape two ¹¹/₁₆" gray balls into 1¹/₄" long tapered logs. Overlap a ¹/₄" two-tone green and a ¹/₄" two-tone pink patch (see page 63 for patch instructions) and press to each arm; make stitch lines with the pin. Press a ⁵/₁₆" peach ball to each arm.

3 **Collar:** Flatten a ⁹/₁₆" pink ball to 1¹/₈" across. Scallop the edge with a toothpick and use the stirrer to stamp each scallop. Place the collar over the neck and shoulders; press a ¹/₄" green patch to the front and use the pin to draw stitches. Cut a ³/₁₆" heart from a ¹/₁₆" thick pink scrap; press it to the patch. Insert a toothpick into her neck to extend ¹/₂". **Head:** Roll a ⁷/₈" peach ball and press onto her neck. Press

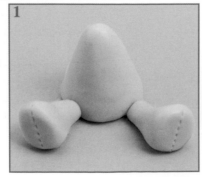

the seed beads for eyes using the pin to make a smile line by each. Use the paintbrush and chalk to blush her cheeks.

4 **Watering can:** Shape a $9/16$" gray ball into a $7/8$" tall cone. Roll two $1/2$" gray balls into two $11/8$" long logs. Shape one for a spout and one for a handle as shown in the diagram; place as shown. Shape a $5/16$" gray ball into a half circle and place on top of the can. Press a $5/8$"x$1/4$" tan and burgundy patch to the can bottom, stitch with a toothpick. Cut a flower from $1/16$" thick yellow clay; cut a teardrop for a leaf from $1/16$" thick green clay. Overlap the leaf with the flower and place

as shown. Add a $1/8$" orange ball for a flower center. Indent the center with a toothpick. Attach the watering can to her front as shown in the large photo on page 56. Bake then antique the project. Seal. **Hair:** Make one pom with four loops from each muslin fabric strip by wrapping strips around index and middle fingers. Slip off fingers, pinch in the middle and secure with wire. Cut loops. Glue the poms in a row over the top of her head. Use the checked fabric strip to make a bow and glue to her hair as shown.

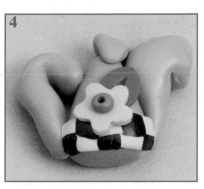

Luvin' Li'l Mini Kitty
by Linda Welsh

First, blend to make:
• stripes: $1/2$" ball of tan + $1/4$" ball of orange

1 **Body:** Shape an $11/16$" tan ball into a $3/4$" wide cone. Use the knife to make a $1/2$" slit up the center. **Feet:** Roll two $1/2$"x$3/8$" tapered logs; indent the bottoms with your thumb as shown. Press one to each side of her body extending wide end forward. Roll two $1/4$" tan balls and press at her body base. Cut two toe lines in each foot as shown. Insert a toothpick to extend $1/2$" from her neck.

2 **Head:** Shape a $9/16$" tan ball into a $1/2$" rounded triangle; cut a $1/8$" long slit for her muzzle; press onto the toothpick for her head. Roll a $1/16$" brown ball; press to the top of her muzzle for a nose. Press the seed beads for eyes and use the pin to indent smile lines. **Ears:** Shape two $3/16$" tan balls into rounded triangles, press one to each side of her head and indent with a pin as shown in the large photo. **Tail:** Roll a $1/8$"x1" tan log; press to her behind and wrap around to her left foot. Pinch a $3/16$" ball of stripe color to a point and press onto the tail tip.

3 **Stripes:** Flatten the remaining pale orange color to $1/16$" thick. Cut seven $1/8$"–$3/16$" triangles for stripes. Cut two $1/4$" circles for hind foot pads. Place as shown. See page 15, step 5 to make three stone-look blue rosebuds. Roll a $3/16$" ball of green clay. Use the toothpick to shave bits from the ball for foliage. Press foliage and rosebuds under her right cheek as shown. Bake (see page 6) then seal.

Sculpey®: tan, stone-look, green, orange, brown
2 black seed beads
basic supplies (see inside the front cover)

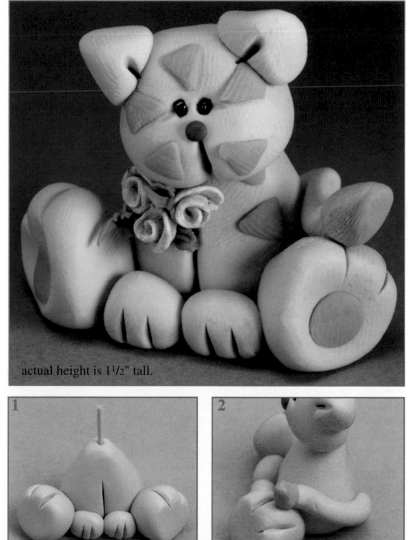

actual height is $11/2$" tall.

Country Kitty Couple

by Linda Welsh

each of these Kitties sit 3¹/8" tall

Sculpey®: orange, peach, burgundy, green, white, black, navy, tan
1³/8"x³/8" piece of tan craft foam
pinking shears
coffee stirrer
six black seed beads
clay cutters: ³/8", ³/16" and ⁵/16" hearts, ³/16"circle
pink powder blush, small paintbrush
black fine-tip permanent-ink pen
basic supplies (see inside the front cover)

First, blend to make:
• fur: 1¹/2" tan ball + 1" orange ball
• stripes: ⁵/8" ball of fur color + ⁷/16" orange ball
• birdhouse, tie, bird's bib: 1" navy ball + ¹/2" white ball

1 *For Her…* **Pantaloons:** Shape two ⁵/8" tan balls into 1" long tapered logs; flatten the tapered ends. Use the side of the pin to press ruffle lines as shown. **Socks:** Press a flattened ⁵/16" green ball to each wide end. **Feet:** Flatten two ¹/2" fur balls; indent two toe lines in each and press one to each sock.

2 **Dress:** Shape a 1¹/4" navy ball into a 1³/8" tall cone. Press the pin side into the bottom edges for ruffles. Angle her legs as shown and press her dress onto them. **Arms:** Roll a ⁵/8" navy ball into a 1" long tapered log. Press a ⁷/16" fur ball to the wide end for a paw; press the other end to her shoulder. Repeat for her other arm. Use the toothpick to poke a hole through her left hand.

3 **Collar:** Flatten tan clay to ¹/16" thick; cut a 1¹/8" circle. Make scallops (see page 7); imprint each with the stirrer. Make cross hatches with the pin and place over her shoulders. Insert a toothpick into her neck to extend ¹/2". **Head:** Shape an ⁷/8" fur ball into a rounded triangle. Use the knife to make a ¹/4" slit in her face bottom for a muzzle. Shape two ⁵/16" fur cones and attach as shown for ears. Press onto the neck toothpick.

4 **Face:** Roll a ¹/16" black ball; press for nose. Press two seed beads for eyes; make whisker dots and brows with the pin. **Stripes:** Flatten stripe clay to ¹/16" thick; cut nine ³/16" long triangles and place as shown. Roll six ¹/16" and two ¹/8" balls; flatten and place for foot pads. **Bow:** Flatten burgundy clay to ¹/8" thick. Cut two ³/8" hearts. Place them, tips-touching, between her ears; press a ¹/16" burgundy ball for a bow center. Indent each with the pin. Make two ³/8" green and tan patches; place as shown making stitch lines with the pin. Cut a ⁵/16" burgundy heart and press it over the collar patch making two button holes with the pin. Cut and press a ³/8" green circle to the dress patch as shown. Bake and seal.

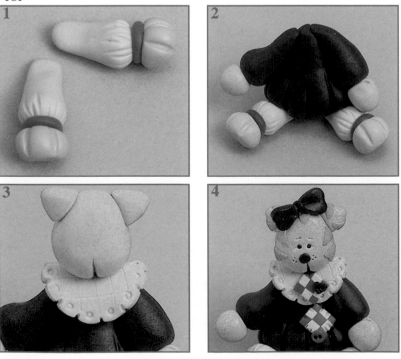

5 *For Him…* **Waist:** Flatten a 1" navy ball to ¹⁄₂" thick. **Legs:** Shape two ³⁄₄" navy balls into ³⁄₄" long logs; press to extend from waist. **Feet:** Shape two ⁵⁄₈" fur balls into ovals, flatten one end for his heel and attach one to each leg. Use the pin to indent two toe lines on each foot.

6 **Body:** Shape a 1¹⁄₈" tan ball into a 1¹⁄₄" tall cone and press onto waist top. **Arms:** Shape two ³⁄₄" tan balls into 1¹⁄₄" long tapered logs; press a ⁷⁄₁₆" fur ball to each wide end for paws and attach a tapered end to each shoulder. Insert a toothpick into his neck to extend ¹⁄₂".

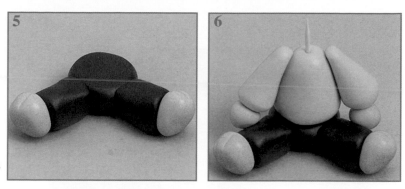

7 **Overalls:** Flatten and cut two ³⁄₁₆x2¹⁄₂"x¹⁄₁₆" bugundy strips. Drape over his shoulders as shown for suspenders. **Head:** Shape a ⁷⁄₈" fur ball into a rounded triangle. **Ears:** Shape two ³⁄₈" fur balls into cones; place as shown. **Face:** Use the knife to make a ¹⁄₄" slit in his face bottom for his muzzle. Press onto the neck toothpick. Roll a ¹⁄₁₆" black ball; press for a nose. Press two seed beads for eyes; make smile lines and brows with the pin. See step 4 to make his stripes and foot pads as for hers.

8 **Bow:** Make a bow as in step 4 using light navy clay; press below his chin. Press a green and tan patch to each arm and make stitch lines with the pin. Use the circle cutter to cut two ¹⁄₁₆" thick burgundy and one ¹⁄₁₆" thick green button. Place the buttons on his shirt as shown.

9 *For her birdhouse:* Shape a ³⁄₄" tan ball into a rounded triangle. Flatten a ⁹⁄₁₆" burgundy ball into a 1¹⁄₄"x⁵⁄₈" oval. Fold for a roof and press it to the birdhouse top. Insert a broken toothpick, jagged end out, into the house front so ¹⁄₈" extends. Flatten navy clay to ¹⁄₁₆" and cut a ³⁄₁₆" heart; press above the bird perch. Press a ¹⁄₄"x⁵⁄₈" green and tan patch below the perch. Cut a ³⁄₁₆" tan circle, press a ³⁄₈" green and tan

patch to the left roof and press the tan button to it, indenting it with the pin head. Set the house on her right leg as shown in the large photo on page 58.

10 *For his birdhouse:* Shape a 1" light navy ball into a rounded triangle; square the sides. Use the pin to draw board lines ¹⁄₈" apart on the front. Flatten a 1¹⁄₂"x⁵⁄₈" burgundy oval. Fold for a roof and press it to the birdhouse top. Press a ³⁄₈" square green and tan patch to each roof side. Cut a ⁵⁄₁₆" tan heart, place as shown and poke two pin holes into it. Use a toothpick to poke a bird hole as shown and insert a broken toothpick, jagged side out of the house for a perch. Press a ¹⁄₄"x1" green and tan patch below it. Set the house between his legs as shown in the large photo on page 58.

11 *For the bird…* **Body:** Shape a ⁵⁄₈" black ball into a rounded triangle; flatten a ¹⁄₄" light navy ball into a teardrop and press it to the bird's body for his bib. Use the pin to make stitch lines. **Feet:** Press two flattened ³⁄₁₆" orange balls to the body bottom and use the pin to indent toes. **Wings:** Roll two ³⁄₈" balls into ¹⁄₂" cones, press to the body and pinch up the tips. **Head:** Shape a ¹⁄₂" black ball into a rounded triangle. Press two black seed beads for eyes and draw brows as shown. Roll a ¹⁄₁₆" orange ball and press it for a beak. Set the bird on his right leg. Bake, then seal (see page 7).

12 Use the pinking shears to trim the ends of the tan craft foam. Use the pen to write "Every Birdie Welcome" on it. Outline the sign with the pen. Trim the top off a toothpick, glue the sign as shown and insert it into her hand.

59

Cat by Shohreh Dolkhani

actual width 3"

Sculpey®: beige, blue, silver, turquoise, green, yellow, black
3"x2¹/2"x1¹/2" wood block
¹/4" square stencil, ¹/2" flat paintbrush, stiff toothbrush
acrylic paints: orange, golden brown, light blue, black, white
#0 liner paintbrush
¹/2" flat paintbrush
pink powder blush
broad-tip black permanent pen
basic supplies (see inside the front cover)

1 **Legs:** Shape four ⁷/16" beige balls into ⁵/8" long tapered logs. Press them together. Push a ¹/2" length of toothpick into each leg, leaving ¹/4" exposed. **Body:** Shape a ³/4" beige ball into an egg. Press onto the legs. Push a ¹/2" length of toothpick into the top front, leaving ¹/4" exposed. **Tail:** Shape a ¹/8"x1¹/2" beige tapered log. Press the wide end onto the rump and curl as shown.

2 **Head:** Shape a ³/4" beige ball into a rounded triangle. Press the wide end onto the body toothpick so it leans back slightly. Blush the cheeks. **Ears:** Shape two ⁵/16" beige balls into rounded triangles. Use a toothpick to indent the base of each, then press one ear onto each side of the head. **Muzzle:** Flatten two ³/16" beige balls to ¹/8" thick. Attach side by side to the lower face. Use the pin to make three whisker dots on each. **Nose:** Shape a ¹/8" black ball into a rounded triangle. Press onto the muzzle top. **Bow:** Roll a ¹/8"x1" blue log and flatten to ¹/16" thick. Fold the ends to the middle, pinch the center and attach to her right ear.

3 **Collar:** Roll a ¹/16"x1¹/2" blue log, flatten and wrap around the neck. **Tag:** Flatten a ³/16" gray ball to ¹/16" thick. Use the pin to make a hole in the top. Press onto the collar. **Bowl:** Flatten a ⁵/8" gray ball to ¹/4" thick. Use your thumb to hollow the center. **Fish:** Shape a ⁷/16" turquoise ball into a teardrop and flatten to ¹/8" thick. Roll a ¹/4" turquoise ball into a curve and flatten to ¹/8" thick; attach for the tail. Flatten two ³/16" turquoise balls into rounded triangles. Attach for fins. Use the knife tip to imprint scale lines and a mouth. **Flower & leaves:** Follow page 63 to make a blue flower and two leaves. Press the flower and leaves together.

4 Bake (see page 6) each piece. Paint eyes (see page 7) on the cat and a simple eye on the fish. Mix two parts water with three parts brown paint. Dip a toothpick into the mixture and whisk it back and forth across the cat to paint a stripe. Repeat for the number of stripes desired. **Base:** Paint the wood block orange. Let dry. Stencil two rows of white checks across the top of one 3"x2¹/2" side; repeat on the bottom. Spatter (see inside the back cover) white, then black paint on the front. Use the fine-tip pen to draw a — ‖ border around the front. Use the broad-tip pen to write "My Cat's Not Spoiled, I'm Just Well Trained" inside the border. Add black dip dots to the ends of the letters. Glue the pieces to the top as shown.

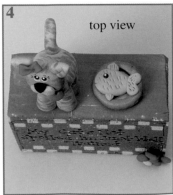

top view

60

Sculpey®: tan, blue, ivory, brown, red, silver, violet, yellow, green, black
3¹/₂"x2¹/₂"x1¹/₂" wood block
acrylic paints: green, light blue, black, white
paintbrushes: ¹/₂" flat, #0 liner brush
¹/₄" square stencil
pink powder blush
stiff toothbrush
broad-tip black permanent pen
basic supplies (see inside the front cover)

Dog by Shohreh Dolkhani

actual width 3¹/₂"

1 Legs: Shape four ¹/₂" tan balls into ¹/₂" long tapered logs and press them together. Push a ¹/₂" length of toothpick into each, leaving ¹/₄" exposed. **Body:** Shape a ⁷/₈" tan ball into an oval and flatten slightly. Press onto the legs. Push a ¹/₂" length of toothpick into the top front, leaving ¹/₄" exposed. **Head:** Shape a ³/₄" tan ball into an egg and flatten slightly. Press the wide end onto the body toothpick, leaning back slightly. Blush the cheeks. **Tail:** Roll a ³/₈" tan ball into a ¹/₂" long tapered log. Press the wide end onto the rump.

2 Ears: Flatten two ⁷/₁₆" tan balls to match the pattern. Blush the inner ears. Pinch the top and bottom of each ear, then press one onto each side of the head. Indent with the side of the pin. **Spots:** Flatten several ¹/₈"–⁵/₁₆" brown balls. Press them onto the body, legs, tail, ears, and head. **Nose:** Flatten a ³/₁₆" black ball to ¹/₈" and shape into a rounded triangle. Press onto the lower head. Use the pin to draw a vertical line under the nose. Make three whisker dots on each cheek.

3 Collar: Roll a ¹/₄" red ball into a 2" long log. Wrap around the neck. **Tag:** Flatten a ³/₁₆" silver ball to ¹/₁₆" thick. Use the pin to make a hole in the top. Press onto the collar, under the head as shown. **Bowl:** Flatten an ¹¹/₁₆" blue ball to ¹/₄" thick. Use your thumb to hollow out the center. **Bones:** Flatten two ⁷/₁₆" ivory balls to ³/₃₂" thick and shape into bones—use the knife to indent the ends and a paintbrush handle to indent the sides. **Flower &**

leaves: See page 63 to make a violet flower and two green leaves. Press together as shown. Bake (see page 6) each piece.

4 Paint eyes (see page 7) on the dog. Base: Paint the wood block green; let dry. Stencil two rows of white checks across the top of one 3¹/₄"x2¹/₄" side; repeat at the bottom. Spatter (see inside the back cover) white, then black paint on the front. Use the fine-tip pen to draw a —‖— border around the front. Use the broad-tip pen to write "Love Me, Love My Dog" inside the border. Add black dip dots to the ends of the letters. Glue the characters to the top of the base as shown. Write your dog's initial on the dog tag.

1 2 3 4 top view

actual height 3½"

Clarence the Clown
by Shohreh Dolkhani

Sculpey®: ivory, red, white, yellow, lime green, violet, blue, neon orange, pale peach
garlic press or Kemper Klaygun
acrylic paint: light blue, black, white
#0 liner paintbrush
pink powder blush, small paintbrush
1" square of cardboard
stiff toothbrush
broad-tip black permanent pen
basic supplies (see inside the front cover)

1 Shoes: Shape two $^9/_{16}$" ivory balls into eggs and flatten them to $^3/_{32}$" thick. Use the pin to indent the sides every $^1/_8$" to create the look of tread. Shape two $^{11}/_{16}$" red balls into eggs and flatten to $^1/_4$" thick. Press them onto the soles. Use the pin to make crosshatch marks on the outside top of each shoe. **Laces:** Roll four $^1/_{16}$"x$^3/_{16}$" white logs and place two on each shoe.

2 Legs: Roll two $^{11}/_{16}$" yellow balls into $^3/_4$" long tapered logs. Press the wide end of each onto the back of a shoe. **Cuffs:** Roll a $^1/_4$"x3" yellow log and flatten to $^1/_{16}$" thick. Wrap around one leg just above the shoe, cut off excess and wrap it around the other leg. Push a $^1/_2$" length of toothpick into each leg, leaving $^1/_4$" exposed. Place the legs side by side.

3 Body: Shape a 1" yellow ball into a rounded triangle. Press onto the legs. Push a $^1/_2$" length of toothpick into the body, leaving $^1/_4$" exposed. Use the pin to draw a # on the lower right front. **Arms:** Roll two $^9/_{16}$" green balls into 1" long tapered logs. Press one onto each side of the body. Press a $^3/_8$" peach ball onto the end of each arm. **Straps:** Roll two $^1/_8$"x1" yellow logs. Flatten to $^1/_{16}$" thick. Wrap over the top of the body as shown, crossing them in back.

4 Head: Shape a $^7/_8$" peach ball into a rounded triangle. Press onto the body. Blush the cheeks. **Nose:** Shape a $^1/_4$" red ball into an oval and press onto the face.

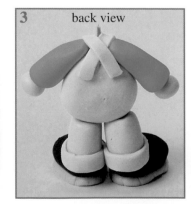

back view

5 **Hair:** Press orange clay through the garlic press to $1/4$"–$1/2$" long; cut off. Use a toothpick to attach the strands to the head as shown, curling them for a natural look. Use two short strands for the eyebrows. **Ears:** Use the pin head to press a $3/16$" peach ball onto each side of the head in front of the hair.

6 **Front pocket:** Roll a $1/4$" blue ball into an oval and flatten to $1/16$" thick. Attach to the overalls below the straps as shown in the large photo on page 62. **Back pocket:** Flatten a $3/16$" blue ball to $1/16$" thick and shape to match the pattern. Press onto his bottom below the left strap. Use the pin to draw stitches around each pocket.

front pocket   back pocket

7 **Flower:** See below to make a violet flower, but use $1/8$" balls of clay. Press the flower onto the left strap front. **Button:** Use the pin head to press a $1/8$" violet ball onto the end of the right strap front. Use the pin to make two holes in the center. Bend his right arm slightly upward and use the side of the pin to crease the inner elbow. Push a toothpick into his right hand, then remove it. Bake (see page 6).

8 Paint his eyes (see page 7). **Sign:** Spatter (see inside the back cover) the cardboard with white paint, then with black. Use the broad-tip pen to write "No Bozos" in the center. Glue one end of a toothpick into the bottom of the sign. Glue the other end into the hole in his hand as shown in the large photo on page 62.

Flowers & Leaves:

Flowers: Place five $3/16$" balls in a circle and flatten slightly. Flatten a $3/16$" yellow ball onto the center. **Leaves:** Flatten three $1/4$" bright green balls and shape. Use the pin to draw the center line.

Making A Patch:

Flatten colors to $1/8$" thick; cut $1/8$" wide strips. 1) Lay strips alongside each other as follows: color A, color B, color A, color B, color A. 2) Cut into $1/8$" wide slices and piece together alternatingly. 3) Cut the patch size.

Sweet Little Mermaid

by Linda Welsh

*Sculpey®: translucent, pale peach, green, blue,
  white, magenta, yellow,
2¹/₄" long clam shell
3 black seed beads
clay cutters: ³/₈" flower,
  ³/₈" and ¹/₄" teardrops
pink chalk, small paintbrush
1¹/₂" length of 24-gauge silver wire
basic supplies (see inside the front cover)*

First, blend an ¹¹/₁₆" ball of blue with an ⁹/₁₆"
ball of white for the blue ocean—knead it only
until it is marbled not fully blended. Repeat to
make a ball for her fin, flowers and fish.

1 **Base:** Roll the blue ocean clay into a ⁵/₁₆"x6" long
log. Flatten and press around the shell bottom for
water. Save a ¹/₂" ball of the second batch of blended
blue for steps 3 and 4. **Fin:** Twist together ³/₁₆"x4"
logs of green magenta and blended blue and knead
until marbled. Shape this into a 2" long tapered log.
Use the pattern to shape the fins. To make scallops
(see page 7), start at the bottom of the fin and work
to the top, indenting to make the scallops seem raised
or embossed. Use the pin to indent folds into the tip.
Insert a toothpick to extend ¹/₂" from her waist. **Body:**
Shape a ⁷/₈" peach ball into a rounded triangle; press
onto her waist. Set her on the shell and curve her
body up; curve her tail fins forward as shown.
Insert a toothpick to extend ¹/₂" from her neck.

2 **Arms:** Shape two ⁵/₈" peach balls into ¹/₄"
long tapered logs. Press a narrow end to each
shoulder as shown; use the stylus to indent wrists.
Head: Roll a ³/₄" peach ball; press onto her neck.
Press two seed beads for eyes; use a pin to indent
lashes and brows. Use the paintbrush and chalk
to blush her cheeks. **Hair:** Use translucent clay
and shape six ⁷/₁₆" balls into 1" logs and two ³/₈"
balls into ³/₄" logs. Flatten each and indent hair
lines with the pin. Shape each into a "C." Press
the curls around her face using the two small
ones for bangs. Overlap the curls as shown. Shape
three ⁵/₈"x1¹/₂" translucent logs. Indent hair lines
and curve slightly. Press to her head back meeting
and overlapping the front curls to cover her head.

3 **Flowers:** Flatten yellow, green, blended
blue, magenta and white clay to ¹/₁₆" thick
each. Cut 5 yellow, 2 green, 1 blue, 5 magenta
and 4 white flowers. Cut eight ³/₈" and three
¹/₄" teardrops for leaves. Indent a vein on each with
the pin. Group as shown in the diagrams and place as
shown in the photo below. Press a ¹/₁₆" ball of clay
as shown to the flower centers and indent each with
the pin.

4 **Fish:** Flatten green, pink and blue clay to ³/₁₆"
thick. Use the pattern to piece together the fish.
Indent the fins and imprint the pattern with the pin
on her body. Press the seed bead for an eye. Coil the
wire around a toothpick and insert one end in front of
his lower fin and the other behind the flower group

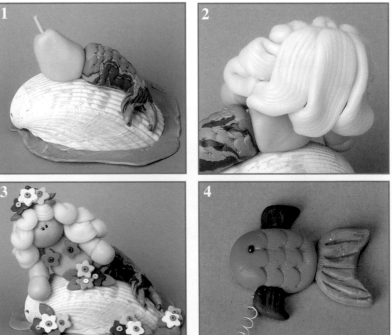

Buttercup Fairy by Linda Welsh

Sculpey®: turquoise, magenta, fluorescent green, dark brown, pale peach, yellow, white
two black seed beads
24-gauge wire: two 2" long yellow, four 4" long black, one 4" long green
clay cutters: 3/16" flower, 3/16" and 5/16" teardrops, 5/16" heart, 1/8" circle
basic supplies (see inside the front cover)

She stands 4" tall.

1 **Shoes:** Flatten two 9/16" turquoise balls, the heel ends lower than the toes, and place side by side. **Socks:** Flatten two 1/4" yellow balls over each shoe and indent the edges with the pin. Flatten and attach two 5/16" turquoise balls. Press a 1/8" magenta ball to each outer ankle and one to each shoe tip. Use a pin to indent four 1/16" green balls; place on her shoe tips for leaves. Press a 1/16" white ball to each flower center; indent with the pin point. Insert a 1" long toothpick into each shoe.

2 **Body:** Shape a 1" magenta ball into a 1 1/4" tall cone. Press the side of the pin along the bottom edge for ruffles. **Pantaloons:** Shape two 7/16"x3/16" turquoise balls. Indent ruffles and press to her body bottom. Press onto her legs slipping one toothpick into each pantaloon—leave a 1/8" space between the body and shoes. **Arms:** Roll two 9/16" turquoise balls into 7/8" long tapered logs. Press a flattened 1/4" yellow ball and a 3/8" peach ball to each wide end; use the pin to poke a hole through each hand. Use the pin to indent ruffles in the sleeve ends and to make tri-dots as shown. Press an arm to each shoulder. Insert a toothpick to extend 1/2" from her neck. **Accents:**

Flatten white and green clay to 1/16". Use the clay cutters to cut a white flower and two green small teardrops. Roll three 1/8" yellow balls. Use the pattern to shape a 1/4" turquoise ball into a pocket. Use the pin to make stitch lines down the center of her dress and poke each button hole; press each accent to her dress front. Press a yellow circle for a pocket flower and two green shavings for leaves. Indent the flower center with the pin.

3 **Head:** Roll a 3/4" peach ball and press it onto her neck. Press the seed beads for eyes and use the pin to make lashes and brows. **Hair:** Flatten brown clay to 1/16" thick, cut a 1 1/8" circle and press to her head. Flatten magenta clay to 1/16" thick; cut a 1/8"x1" strip and two hearts. Wrap the strip over her hair for a headband, press the hearts, points together, for a bow and press a 1/8" magenta ball in the center. Indent with the pin as shown. Shape two 1/2" brown balls for ponytails and press as shown. Roll three 1/8"x1/2" brown logs. Place for bangs and curve each as shown. Trim the center bang to 1/8".

4 **Swag:** Flatten green clay to 1/16" thick; cut five 5/16" teardrops and use the pin side to indent the leaves. Group five 1/4" white balls for the center flower; group eight 3/16" white balls for the two end flowers. Roll 1/8" yellow balls for flower centers. Blend (see page 6) turquoise and white clay; roll six 1/16" balls; poke holes in each and place as shown. Flatten a 5/16" white ball and press to the center flower back. Thread the green wire between the two and remove it. **Wings:** Use your fingers to shape the yellow and black wires to follow the patterns. Poke the wings and antennae in place and remove them. Brush chalk on her cheeks. Bake. Insert the green wire into the floral swag and use your fingers to coil the wire, thread one end through each hand and twist the ends to secure. Glue and insert wings and antennae. Seal.

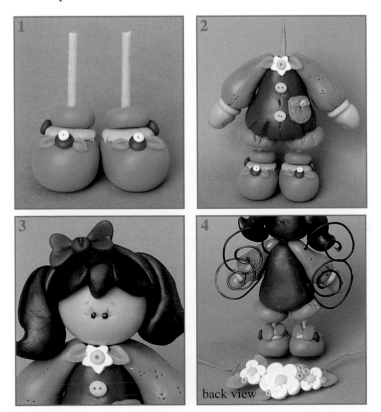

back view

65

Hawg Wash by Linda Welsh

Sculpey®: pale peach, white, red
4"x1¹/₂"x1³/₄" white-flecked blue miniature bath tub
1¹/₂" square of blue checked fabric
1¹/₂"x2" piece of burgundy print fabric
¹/₂"x6" strip of burgundy checked fabric
³/₄" tall miniature wooden milk bottle
3mm pearl beads: 400
6 black seed beads
12" of 22-gauge wire, soft cloth
dark brown acrylic paint
pink chalk, small paintbrush
black fine-tipper manent-ink pen
jewelry glue (such as E6000™ or Goop®)
basic supplies (see inside the front cover)

ear

actual height is 2³/₄"
without wire handle.

1 **Tub:** Press a 1³/₄" ball of scrap clay into the bottom of the tub for filler. Flatten a 1" ball of white clay into an oval shape and stretch over the filler for water. Insert a toothpick into the front tub center and one on the right and left sides. **Soap:** Blend (see page 6) a ¹/₁₆" red ball, a ¹/₂" peach ball and a ¹/₂" white ball. Flatten to ³/₁₆" and cut a ¹/₄"x⁷/₁₆" piece; set aside for step 3. **Center Hawg's Behind:** Roll a ³/₄" peach ball. Indent one side with a toothpick and place it in the rear center of the tub. **Tail:** Roll a ¹/₁₆"x³/₄" peach log, coil around a toothpick and press it to the top of his behind. **Arms:** Roll two ⁵/₈" peach balls into 1" long tapered logs. Flatten the bottom and indent the wide end with a toothpick for hooves. Trim the center toothpick to 1" long. Place arms ¹/₄" apart in the center front of the tub hanging over the tub edge.

2 **Center Head:** Roll a ⁷/₈" peach ball into a rounded triangle and push it onto the center toothpick overlapping his arms. **Left Body:** Roll a ⁹/₁₆" peach ball into a ¹/₂" cone; push onto the left toothpick. Trim toothpick to extend ³/₈". **Arms:** Roll two ⁹/₁₆" peach balls into ³/₄" long tapered logs; flatten the bottom and indent the wide end with a toothpick for hooves. Press one to each side of his body. **Head:** Roll a ⁵/₈" peach ball into a rounded triangle; press onto his body. **Right Body:** Roll a ⁵/₈" peach ball into a ⁵/₈" rounded triangle; push onto the right toothpick. Trim toothpick to extend ³/₈". **Arms:** Roll two ⁹/₁₆" peach balls into 1" long tapered logs; flatten the bottom and indent the wide end with a toothpick for hooves. Press one to each side of his body. **Head:** Roll an ¹¹/₁₆" peach ball into a rounded triangle; press onto his body. **Ears:** Roll six ³/₈" peach balls and flatten into ⁵/₈" long triangles as shown on the pattern. Place an ear on each upper side of a hog head folding the ear tips forward. **Snout:** Flatten a ³/₈" peach ball to a ³/₈"x¹/₂" oval; press to each face. Poke two holes with a toothpick for nostrils.

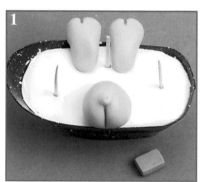

3 Press two seed beads above each snout for eyes; use a toothpick to draw lashes and brows as shown. Use the paintbrush and chalk to blush each cheek and the center hawg's behind. Loosely coil the wire around the paintbrush handle and insert one end into each tub side as shown. Bake the tub and soap.

4 Cover the tub water with glue allowing some to drip over the outer edges and on the hawgs' heads. Sprinkle pearl beads into the glue for bubbles. Antique then seal. Use the fabric strip to make a bow and secure it to the tub handle with wire as shown. Fold the fabric pieces into "towels." Write "HAWG Wash" on the miniature bottle. Glue the bottle, towels and soap in front of the tub as shown in the large photo above.

actual width 3"

Happy Hogs
by Shohreh Dolkhani

Sculpey®: pale peach, bright green, dark green, violet, yellow
1¹/2"x1" piece of cardboard
acrylic paints: light blue, black, white
#0 paintbrush
pink powder blush, small paintbrush
stiff toothbrush
broad-tip black permanent pen
basic supplies (see inside the front cover)

1 **Base:** Flatten a 1¹/8" bright green ball to match the pattern. **Mommy Pig:** Shape four ¹/4"x¹/2" peach logs for legs. Use the pin to imprint hoof lines. Press the legs together as shown. Push a ¹/2" length of toothpick into each, leaving ¹/4" exposed. **Body:** Shape a ³/4" peach ball into an egg and press onto the legs. **Head:** Shape a ⁵/8" peach ball into a rounded triangle. Press onto the body top.

2 Blush the cheeks. **Muzzle:** Shape a ⁵/16" peach ball into an oval and flatten to ¹/8" thick. Press onto the lower front of the head. Use the pin head to imprint nostrils.

3 **Ears:** Push two ¹/2" toothpick lengths into the head, leaving ¹/4" of each exposed. Flatten two ³/8" peach balls. Blush one side of each. Pinch the top and bottom of each. Press one onto each toothpick. **Tail:** Roll a ¹/16"x¹/2" peach log. Press one end onto

the back of the body and coil. Attach Mommy to the right front base as shown.

4 **Daddy Pig:** Make as for Mommy Pig, but attach at the left. **Baby Pig:** Make as for Mommy Pig, but use the following sizes: legs: ³/16"x¹/4"; body—⁹/16"; head—¹/2"; muzzle—³/16"; ears—¹/4"; tail—³/16". Attach between Mommy and Daddy. **Flower & leaf:** See page 63 to make a violet flower and a dark green leaf. Attach to the base as shown. **Sign support:** Flatten a ¹/4" bright green ball onto the back of the base. Push a toothpick into the center, then remove. Bake (see page 6). Paint the eyes (see page 7). **Sign:** Spatter (see inside the back cover) the cardboard with white, then with black paint. Let dry. Use the broad-tip pen to write "Happy As Hogs" on the cardboard. Make black dip dots on the ends of the letters. Glue a toothpick into the lower bottom. Glue the other end of the toothpick into the hole in the support.

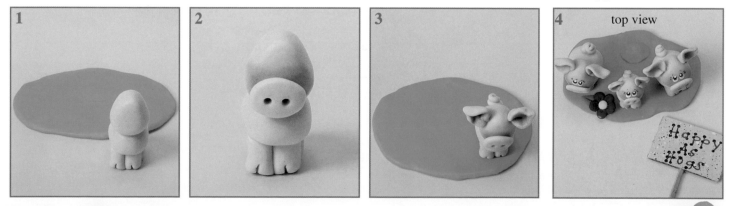

Noah & Friends
by Shohreh Dolkhani

*Sculpey®: tan, brown, black,
 pale peach, beige, green,
 gray, white, pink, stone-look
 blue, stone-look green, yellow*
5¹/₂"x2¹/₂"x1¹/₂" wood block
*acrylic paints: brown, light
 blue, black, white*
paintbrushes: ¹/₂" flat, #0 liner
*garlic press or Kemper
 Klaygun*
pink powder blush
¹/₄" square stencil
floral moss
stiff toothbrush
broad-tip black permanent pen
*basic supplies (see inside the
 front cover)*

actual width 5¹/₂"

1 Noah…Sandles/Feet: Shape two ⁵/₈" tan balls into teardrops and flatten. Repeat with two ⁵/₁₆" peach balls; press one onto each sandal. Roll four ¹/₁₆"x³/₄" tan logs. Pinch the ends of two together and press onto a sandal front, then wrap one over the foot to each side. Repeat for the other sandal. Press five ³/₁₆"–¹/₈" peach balls onto the front of each foot for toes.

2 Legs: Shape two ⁷/₁₆" peach balls into ³/₈" long logs. Press one onto the top back of each foot. Push a ¹/₂" length of toothpick into each leg, leaving ¹/₄" exposed. Place the legs side by side.

3 Cloak: Shape a 1¹/₈" stone-look green ball into a cone. Press onto the legs. Push a ¹/₂" length of toothpick into the top, leaving ¹/₄" exposed. Use the pin to draw a # on the bottom right corner. **Buttons:** Use the pin head to press two ³/₁₆" tan balls onto the cloak front. Use the pin point to make two holes in each.

4 Arms: Shape two ⁹/₁₆" stone-look green balls into 1" long tapered logs. Press a ⁵/₁₆" peach ball onto the end of each, then attach one to each side of the body as shown. **Head:** Shape a ⁷/₈" peach ball into an egg. Press onto the body. Blush his cheeks.

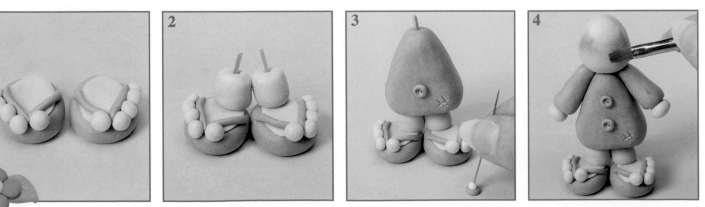

5 **Beard:** Shape a $7/16$"x1" white log. Roll each end to a blunt point, curve and flatten to $3/32$" thick. Wrap around his chin as shown. **Mustache:** Shape two $1/4$" white balls into teardrops and flatten to $1/16$" thick. Press onto the head above the beard. **Nose:** Shape a $3/16$" peach ball into an egg. Press onto the top of the mustache.

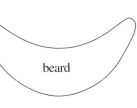

beard

6 **Ears:** Press a $3/16$" peach ball above each end of the beard. Use the head of the pin to indent each ear. **Eyebrows:** Roll two $1/8$" white balls into $3/16$" long logs and flatten. Press one onto each side of the face, $3/8$" above the nose.

7 **Headdress:** Flatten a $7/8$" beige ball to $1/16$" thick and shape into a $1 3/4$"x$2 1/4$" rectangle. Trim the corners to match the pattern. Drape over the top of his head, letting it hang down his back. **Rope:** Roll a $1/16$"x2" brown rope and a $1/16$"x2" tan rope. Twist together. Wrap around the top of the head over the headdress, joining the ends in back.

headdress

8 **Dove:** Shape a $7/16$" stone-look blue ball into an egg. Shape two $3/16$" stone-look blue balls into teardrops. Press one onto each side of the body. Shape a $5/16$" stone-look blue ball into an egg and press onto the top of the first egg. Flatten two $1/8$" yellow balls and press onto the bottom for feet. Shape a $1/8$" yellow ball into a cone and attach for a beak. Blush the dove's face and tummy. Push a $1/2$" length of toothpick into Noah's right hand, leaving $1/4$" exposed. Lift the arm gently up as shown, using the knife to imprint an elbow crease. Press the dove onto the toothpick.

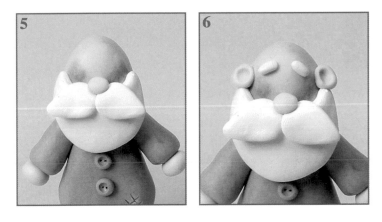

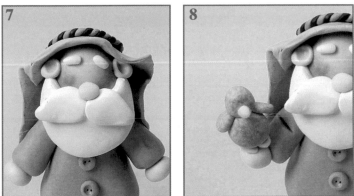

9 **Lion:** Follow page 52, steps 1–2. Press a $3/8$" tan ball onto the lower back body for a back paw. Use the pin to draw toe lines.

10 **Lamb:** Follow page 52, step 3.

11 **Snake:** Shape a $5/8$" green ball into a 3" long tapered log. Coil as shown. Shape a $1/8$" pink ball into an oval, flatten and press onto the large end as shown for a nose.

12 Bake (see page 6) each piece separately. Paint eyes (see page 7) on each character. **Base:** Paint the wood block brown. Let dry. Stencil $1/4$" white blocks in a checkerboard pattern across one $5 1/2$"x$1 1/2$" side. Spatter white paint on the front. Repeat with black. Use the fine-tip pen to draw a — ‖— border around the front. Use the broad-tip pen to write "God Keeps His Promises" inside the border. Make black dip dots on the ends of the letters. Glue all the characters except the snake to the top of the base as shown. Glue moss around them. Glue the snake into the moss.

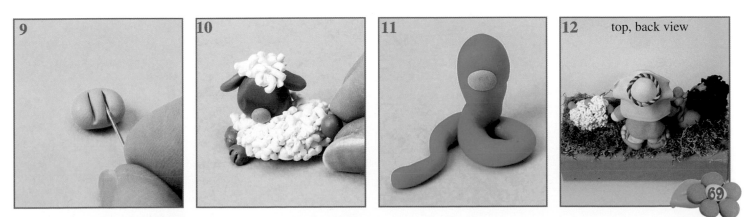

top, back view

Happy Haunting

by Shelly Comiskey

Sculpey®: pale peach, green, white, orange
2 black glass seed beads
one 3" long wood sign cut out
ivory acrylic paint
#8 flat paintbrush
transfer paper
permanent black marker
talcum powder
two 3/4" wide button magnets (or 2" long pin back)
basic supplies (see inside the front cover)

1 Lightly coat the wood sign with talcum. **Arms:** Roll a 1" orange ball into a 2½" long log. Press to the top of the sign and flatten the ends. **Head:** Shape a 1⅛" peach ball into a pear. Push up the center of the wide end with your thumb, emphasizing his chin. Use the side of the paintbrush handle to indent the cleft. Press the top of the head flat. Attach the back center of the head to the center of the arms.

2 **Hands:** Flatten two ⅝" peach balls to ⅜" thick. Use the knife to make three ⅜" long slices in each. Round off the ends of each section to make fingers. Press one hand to the end of each arm to hang over the sign front. Gently arrange the fingers, making sure that each "thumb" touches the face. Use the round end of the pin to indent the end of each finger. Mix a 3/16" peach ball with a 3/16" white ball and press a 1/16" ball of this color into each indent.

3 **Face:** Press a ¼" peach ball onto each side of the head for ears. Use the round end of the pin to indent. Insert the seed beads (see page 7) for eyes. Use the pin to draw eyelashes around the eyes. Use the pin to lightly draw the mouth line, then rock the pin sideways along the mouth line to create a deep slash. Roll a ¼" peach ball into a 1" long log. Flatten the ends and attach for the brow. Attach a ¼" peach ball for the nose. Shape a 1/8" white ball into a triangle and press to one side of the mouth for the tooth. **Hair:** Shape a ⅝" green ball into a ⅜" thick rectangle that fits the top of the head. Press to the top of the head. Use the pin to indent many hairs. Draw a scar on his right cheek. Draw another scar above his brow and seven dots on each side of the scar.

4 Bake (see page 6). Let cool, then gently remove from the sign. Paint the sign ivory; let dry. Trace the pattern onto tracing paper. Transfer it onto the sign. Trace with the marker; let dry. Glue the figure to the sign as shown in the large photo. Glue the magnets or pin back to the back of the sign.

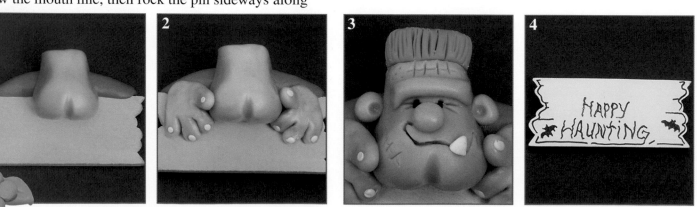

Trick or Treat

by Shelly Comiskey

Sculpey®: ecru, white, sweet potato, maroon, green, gold
5"x10" piece cheesecloth fabriclay (see page 7—use white clay, roll to #4, add the cheesecloth and roll to #5)
1½"x2½" piece of beige cardstock
black fine-tip permanent gel pen
orange acrylic paint
4 size 15/0 black seed beads
red & brown chalks
basic supplies (see inside the front cover)

actual height 3½"

1 **Body**: Shape a ⅞" ecru ball into a pear. Insert ½ of a toothpick into the top so ¼" extends and attach a ¾" ecru ball for the head. Roll a ¼" ecru ball into an oval and attach for the nose. Insert two seed beads for eyes. Use the pin to draw the smile and a vertical crease above each eye.

2 Cut the fabriclay into ¼" wide strips—neatness isn't important! Wrap a strip around the body, leaving gaps where the clay shows through. Wrap more strips as needed to cover the entire body and head, gluing where the strips overlap. Leave the eyes and nose uncovered.

3 **Legs**: Roll two ¾" ecru balls into tapered logs; press the large ends upward to form feet. Roll two ecru balls each of the following sizes: ⅛", ³⁄₁₆", ¼", and ⁵⁄₁₆". Attach as shown for toes. **Arms**: Roll two ⅝" ecru balls into tapered logs. Wrap the arms and legs with fabriclay strips, leaving the heels, toes and most of the arms visible. Attach the legs extending outward and the arms at the shoulders, securing each with glue. Bend the arms as shown.

4 **Pumpkin**: Roll a ¾" ball of sweet potato. Press it onto the table to flatten the bottom and narrow the top. Use the pin to draw vertical segment lines, a smile and eyebrows. Insert two seed beads for eyes. Roll a ¼" maroon ball into an oval and attach for the nose. Use the stylus to poke a hole in the center top. Shape a ³⁄₁₆" gold ball into a cone and insert the point into the hole. Shape two ³⁄₁₆" green balls into ovals, flatten and press one on each side of the stem. Indent with the side of the pin.

(Refer to the large photo.) Blush the pumpkin's cheeks red and the mummy's nose and toes brown, then randomly brush brown chalk over the wrappings. Place the pumpkin between the mummy's legs. Press his right hand onto the pumpkin and curve the left to hold the sign. Bake (see page 6); let cool. **Sign**: Trace and cut out the patterns. Lay on the cardstock and trace with the pen. Cut just outside the traced lines. Draw woodgrain lines. Write "Trick or Treat Smell My Feet!" on the sign. Use the toothpick to apply clusters of three orange dots among the letters. Glue the sign to the stick crosswise, ¹⁄₂" below the top. Glue into the mummy's hand.

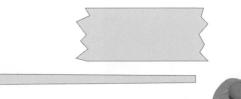

actual height 2¾"

Halloween Friends
by Shohreh Dolkhani

Sculpey®: white, pink, brown, black, orange, green
acrylic paints: light blue, black, white
#0 paintbrush
pink powder blush
basic supplies (see inside the front cover)

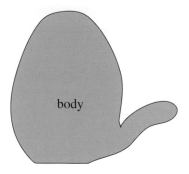

body

1 **Ghost:** Shape a 1¹/₈" white ball into a rounded triangle. Flatten the bottom so it will stand and pinch out a ³/₄" long "tail" at one side. Push a ¹/₂" length of toothpick into the top with ¹/₄" extending. Shape a ³/₄" white ball into a rounded triangle and press onto the toothpick. Blush the cheeks. Roll a ¹/₈" pink ball into an oval and attach for the nose. Use a toothpick to hollow an oval mouth. Roll a ¹/₄" white ball into a long teardrop and attach to the head, curving the tip as shown. Shape two ¹/₂" white balls into tapered logs. Attach to the body sides and use your thumb to indent the ends.

2 **Cat:** Roll four ¹/₄"x³/₈" black logs. Arrange upright in a square for legs. Insert a ¹/₂" toothpick length into the top of each. Shape an ¹¹/₁₆" black ball into an egg. Attach over the legs. Push a ¹/₂" length of toothpick into the top front. Shape a ¹/₂" black ball into a rounded triangle and press onto the toothpick. Roll a ¹/₈"x1" black rope, attach to the rump and curve into an S.

3 Roll two ¹/₄" black balls and attach to the lower face for a muzzle. Use a pin to poke whisker holes. Pinch a ¹/₈" pink ball into a rounded triangle and attach to the muzzle top. Shape two ¹/₄" black balls into triangles. Indent the fronts with a knife. Attach to the top sides of the head.

4 **Pumpkin:** Shape a ⁷/₈" orange ball into a rounded triangle. Use the pin head to indent a hole on the top. Use the knife to draw vertical stripes on the pumpkin. Shape a ¹/₄" green ball into a leaf. Insert into the hole on the pumpkin top. Shape a ³/₁₆" brown ball into a tapered log and attach next to the leaf for a stem. Use toothpick pieces to attach the cat and pumpkin to the ghost as shown in the large photo above. Bake (see page 6). Paint eyes (see page 7) on the cat and ghost.

top view

72

turkey sits 2¼" tall

Talkin' Turkey

by Linda Welsh

Sculpey®: brown, orange, green, red, yellow
30" length of ½" wide orange and black checked fabric
fine-tip permanent-ink pens: black, brown soft cloth, 10" of 24-gauge black wire clay cutters:
  ³/8" flower, ³/4" and ⁵/16" teardrops
dark brown acrylic paint
tan craft foam
pinking shears
2 black seed beads
basic supplies (see inside the front cover)

1 Base: Flatten green clay to ¹/8" thick; cut five ³/4" teardrops for leaves. Indent veins with the pin as shown on the pattern; place as arranged in the diagram. **Pumpkins:** Roll three ⁹/16", one ¹¹/16" and one 1⅛" orange balls. Use the toothpick to indent crease lines. Arrange on the base as shown. Flatten green clay to ¹/16", cut five ³/16" teardrops for leaves and indent a vein on each. Press to the smaller pumpkins as shown. Cut four ¹/2" toothpick pieces, paint them brown and let dry. Insert one into each small pumpkin.

2 For the Turkey… Body: Shape an ¹¹/16" brown ball into a rounded triangle; use the pin to draw "feathers" on his body working upward from the bottom. **Feet:** Roll brown clay ¹/8" thick and cut two flowers. Poke a hole through each and bake (see page 7) for 10 minutes. Set aside for step 4. **Wings:** Shape two ³/8" brown balls into ¹/2" long teardrops. Flatten slightly, press a wing to each shoulder and use a toothpick to indent feathers and draw lines as shown. **Head:** Shape a ¹/2" brown ball into a rounded triangle and press to his body. Press the seed beads for eyes. Shape a ¹/16" orange ball into a triangle and press for a beak; roll a ¹/8" long red log and curve around his beak. Sit the turkey on the large pumpkin.

3 Flowers: Flatten green clay to ¹/8" thick; cut a ³/4" teardrop and use the pattern to indent veins. Tuck the leaf left of the turkey as shown. Flatten yellow clay to ¹/16" thick and cut nine flowers. Press the flowers among the pumpkins as shown; press one to the turkey s lapel. Flatten green clay to ¹/16" thick and cut three ⁵/16" teardrops; indent a vein on each and place one under his lapel flower and the other two among the cluster of flowers right of him. Roll and press a ¹/8" to ¹/16" brown ball to each flower center; indent the lapel flower center with the pin.

4 Sign: Notch and insert the toothpick just behind the left pumpkin, then remove it and the pumpkin stems. Bake. Glue and replace the toothpick and stems. See step 4, page 83 to thread and insert the legs. Use the pattern above to cut and draw the sign from craft foam. Glue it to the post. Antique the clay pieces then seal. **Plumes:** Cut the fabric into 10" lengths; make a 4-loop pom pom (see page 5 wrapped around three fingers from each. Glue to his back.

73

Crawford Crow & Buddy by Judy Ferrill

Sculpey®: black, gold, ivory, white, lilac, sea green
1¹/₂" wide straw hat
acrylic paint: black, white, red; #0 liner brush
garlic press or Kemper Klaygun
#3 wide white perle cotton or heavy white carpet thread
four ¹/₄" wide white buttons with 2 holes
black permanent marking pen
basic supplies (see inside the front cover)

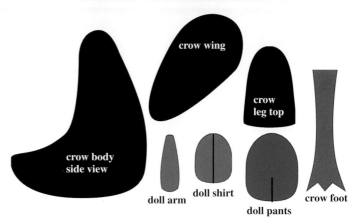

1 **Crow's body:** Shape a 1¹/₈" black ball into a 1¹/₂" tall cone. Pinch and turn up a tail as shown in the side view pattern. Roll a ³/₄" black ball for the head; attach (see page 7). Pinch a ¹/₄" gold ball into a cone and attach for his beak. Use a toothpick to draw nostrils and a mouth line.

2 **Wings:** Flatten and shape two ⁵/₈" black balls to match the pattern. Use the knife edge to imprint feather lines along the edge. **Legs:** Shape two ⁵/₈" black balls into rounded cones, matching the leg top pattern. Imprint as for the wings. Shape two ¹/₄"x1¹/₄" gold logs, flatten one end of each and notch to form toes. Turn the toes up. Imprint horizontal lines. Attach one to the flat end of each leg top.

3 **Scarecrow doll:** Flatten a ¹/₂" green ball to match the pants pattern. Press the side of a toothpick into the bottom to divide the legs. Shape a ³/₈" lilac ball into an oval and press onto the top of the pants. Use the toothpick to draw a center line. Shape two ³/₈" lilac balls to match the arm pattern and attach to the shoulders. Roll a ³/₈" ivory ball and attach for the head.

4 Load the garlic press with ivory and press out ¹/₄" lengths to cover the doll's head, hands and feet. Flatten a ¹/₄" black ball to ¹/₂" across and attach for his hat brim. Attach a ¹/₄" black ball for the crown of the hat. Pierce, bake, finish and assemble (see inside the back cover) the crow. Lay the doll flat to bake. Use the pen to draw eyes, a mouth and sleeve patches on the doll. Paint a red triangle for his nose. After assembling the crow, glue the doll and the straw hat in place as shown in the large photo.

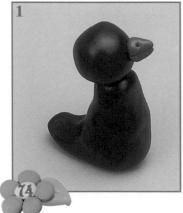

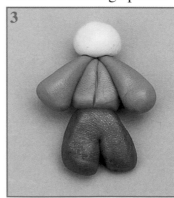

Symon Scarecrow
by Judy Ferrill

Sculpey®: white, ivory, blue, beige, orange, black, violet, sea green, apricot
1¹/₂" wide straw hat
acrylic paint: black, white
#0 line paintbrush
garlic press or Kemper Klaygun
#3 wide white perle cotton or heavy white carpet thread
four ¹/₄" wide white buttons with 2 holes
black permanent marking pen
basic supplies (see inside the front cover)

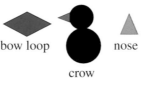

bow loop

crow

nose

1 **Body:** Shape a 1¹/₈" ivory ball into a 1¹/₂" tall cone. Flatten violet to ¹/₁₆" thick and cut a 3"x1¹/₂" rectangle. Wrap it around the lower body so ¹/₂" extends below. Trim excess in back, fold the front under and smooth the seams. Use your finger to indent the front. Cut two ³/₈" squares and attach for pockets. Cut two ¹/₈"x2" violet strips and attach as shown for suspenders. Cut two ³/₈" squares and attach for pockets. Flatten four ³/₁₆" seagreen balls; attach for front and back suspender buttons. Use the tip of a toothpick to imprint button holes and stitches around the pockets.

2 **Head:** Roll a ⁷/₈" beige ball and follow the general directions to attach. Flatten apricot to ¹/₁₆" and cut a triangular nose; attach to the center of the face. Make the ivory hair (see inside the front cover). **Bow tie:** Flatten green to ¹/₁₆" and cut two bow loops. Fold each in half and attach point to point under his chin. Roll a ¹/₁₆" green ball and attach for the knot.

3 **Arms:** Roll two ³/₈"x1¹/₂" ivory logs. Flatten blue to ¹/₁₆" and cut two ¹/₄"x³/₈" patches. Attach and imprint as for the pockets. **Legs:** Make as for the arms, but use violet clay with green clay for the patches. Attach ivory hair to the bottoms of the arms and legs.

4 Press the straw hat onto his head to make an imprint; remove. Pierce the body, arms and legs (see inside the back cover). **Crows:** Shape a ³/₈" black ball for the body and attach a ¹/₄" black ball for the head. Pinch a ¹/₈" orange ball to a point and attach for the beak. Use a toothpick to imprint eyes. Attach to the scarecrow's left foot as shown. Repeat for another crow. Press onto the hat brim, imprinting him to fit; remove. Bake, finish and assemble. Use the pen to draw a curved mouth with stitches. Glue on the hat; glue the second crow to the hat brim.

actual height 2½"

Happy Fall

by Anita Behnen

Sculpey®: sweet potato, translucent
acrylic paints: black, metallic gold, brown,
*   dark green*
1½"x½" piece of white cardstock
2" wide terra cotta pot
½ of a 1" Styrofoam® ball
one 2½" long wired wood floral pick
three to four 18" long strands of raffia
2" tuft of sheet moss
red chalk
1/16" hole punch
3" of dark green metallic yarn
pink powder blush, small paintbrush
black fine-tip permanent gel pen
paper plate
stiff toothbrush
newspapers
basic supplies (see inside the front cover)

1 Spread waxed paper or newspapers to protect your work surface; place the pot in the center. Pour a ½" puddle of gold paint on the paper plate. Dip the bristles of the toothbrush into the paint, point the top of the toothbrush towards the pot and run your thumb over the bristles, spattering the pot with paint. Turn the pot and spatter again; repeat until it s evenly speckled. Spatter again with brown paint, then with green. Let dry.

2 Glue the foam half ball into the pot, flat side up. Glue moss to cover the foam.

3 **Sign**: Trim the edges of the cardstock in random zig-zags (or trim with pattern-edged scissors). Use your finger to rub brown paint on the sign, creating a streaky wood grain. Let dry. Use the black pen to write "Happy Fall Y all." Punch two holes ¼" apart at the top center. Run the floral pick wires through the holes and wrap them securely around the top of the pick. Insert it into the back of the pot.

4 **Large pumpkin**: Shape a ¾" sweet potato ball into an egg. Use your thumb to flatten the top slightly. Use the pin to draw eight segment lines from the center top to the center bottom, more or less evenly spaced.

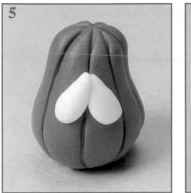

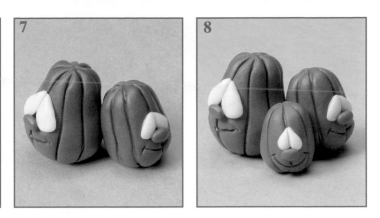

5 **Eyes:** Shape two ³⁄₁₆" balls of translucent clay into teardrops and flatten slightly. Attach over a segment line, points upward, tipped together as shown. The bottom of the eyes should be about halfway down the pumpkin. If the line between the eyes starts to blend, use the pin to redraw it.

6 **Nose:** Shape a ³⁄₁₆" sweet potato ball into a slight oval and press onto the face, barely overlapping the bottom of the eyes. Mouth: Use the pin to draw a squiggly smile below the nose. Draw short dimple lines across each end.

7 **Medium pumpkin**: Follow steps 4–6, but use a ⁵⁄₈" ball of sweet potato for the body and ¹⁄₈" balls of translucent and sweet potato for the eyes and the nose. Press the two pumpkins together so they face away from each other at right angles.

8 **Small pumpkin:** Follow steps 4–6, but use a ¹⁄₂" ball of sweet potato for the body. Use ³⁄₃₂" balls of translucent and sweet potato for the eyes and the nose. Press the small pumpkin against the first two so he faces forward between them.

9 Use the stylus to poke a ¹⁄₈" deep hole in the top of each pumpkin. Blush the cheeks and noses. Bake (see page 6); let cool.

10 Dip the end of the stylus into black paint and dot black pupils on the eyes of the large and medium pumpkins. Use the pin to dot the eyes on the small pumpkin. Let dry. Use the pin to highlight each eye with a tiny metallic gold dot.

11 **Hair**: Cut five 1½" yarn lengths. Hold two together, fold in half and glue the fold into the hole of the large pumpkin. Repeat for the medium pumpkin. Fold the last strand in half and glue into the hole of the small pumpkin. Let the glue dry, then fray the yarn and trim as desired.

12 Hold the raffia strands together and wrap around the rim of the pot. Secure with a dab of glue at the back of the pot, then tie in the front, making a shoestring bow (see inside the back cover) with ¾" loops and 2" tails. Glue the pumpkins into the moss in front of the sign as shown in the large photo on page 76.

Patience Pilgrim
by Judy Ferrill

Sculpey®: terra cotta, ivory, beige, orange, black, white, green
clay cutters: 3/16" and 1/4" hearts, 1/2" teardrop (or use the patterns below)
acrylic paint: black, white; #0 liner brush
garlic press or Kemper Klaygun
#3 wide white perle cotton or heavy white carpet thread
four 1/4" wide white buttons with 2 holes
black permanent marking pen
basic supplies (see inside the front cover)

bonnet

bow loop   shoe

Bonnet: Flatten a 5/8" ivory ball to 11/8" across. Shape it into a dome and attach to the top of her head. Use a toothpick to draw seam lines as shown on the pattern. From the flattened ivory, cut a 3/16"x2" strip and attach across the front for a brim. **Tie:** From the flattened black, cut two bow loops and two 1/8"x3/4" strips for tails. Attach the tails below her chin, angling slightly apart. Fold the loops in half and attach them point to point over the top of the tails. Roll a 1/16" black ball and press into the center for a knot.

3 Arms: Roll two 3/8"x11/2" maroon logs. Roll two 3/8" beige balls and attach one to the lower end of each arm. From the flattened white cut two 3/16"x2" strips and wrap for cuffs. **Pumpkin:** Roll a 5/8" orange ball. Use a toothpick to draw segment lines. Roll a 1/8" thick green rope, cut a 1/4" length and attach for the stem. Attach the pumpkin to her right hand.

4 Legs: Shape two 1/2" ivory balls into 5/8" tall cones. Roll two 1/4"x1" beige logs and attach one to the flat end of each cone. From the flattened white cut two 3/16"x2" strips. Scallop the top edges and wrap around the leg bottoms for socks. **Shoes:** Roll two 9/16" black balls into ovals, slightly flatten one end of each and attach the flattened ends at the bottoms of the legs. Pierce, bake and finish (see inside the back cover); use the black pen to add a smile. Assemble.

1 Body: Shape a 11/8" terra cotta ball into a 11/2" tall cone. **Apron:** Flatten ivory to 1/16" and cut a 31/4"x1" piece. Scallop (see page 7) the lower edge and both short edges. Use the heart cutters to remove a large heart with a small heart to its right. Wrap around the body with the scallops even with the bottom edge. Cut a 1/4"x3/8" ivory pocket and attach on the right side. Use the tip of a toothpick to imprint stitches around the pocket and gather lines at the apron top. **Collar:** Cut two teardrops, scallop each and attach with the points forward as shown.

2 Head: Roll a 3/4" beige ball and follow the general directions to attach it to the body. Roll a 1/16" biege ball and attach for her nose. Make terra cotta hair.

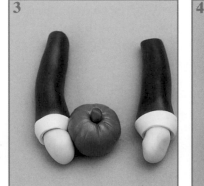

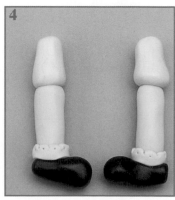

Parker Pilgrim by Judy Ferrill

Sculpey®: terra cotta, chocolate, ivory, beige, red,
  black, orange, green
acrylic paint: black, white; #0 liner brush
garlic press or Kemper Klaygun
#3 wide white perle cotton or heavy white carpet thread
four ¹/₄" wide white buttons with 2 holes
black permanent marking pen
basic supplies (see inside the front cover)

collar

1 **Body:** Shape a 1¹/₈" ball of terra cotta into a 1⁵/₈" tall cone. Use the knife to imprint a line down the center front. **Pants:** Flatten black to ¹/₁₆" thick and cut a 3"x1¹/₂" rectangle. Wrap it around the lower body so ¹/₂" extends below. Trim excess in back, fold the front under and smooth the seams. Use your finger to indent the front. Cut two ³/₈" squares and attach for pockets. Make stitching dots with the toothpick. **Collar:** Flatten ivory to ¹/₁₆" thick and cut two. Place side by side, curving them slightly as shown.

2 **Head:** Roll a ³/₄" beige ball and attach (see page 7) it to the body. Roll a ¹/₁₆" beige ball and attach for his nose. Make terra cotta hair. **Hat:** Flatten a ¹/₂" black ball to ⁷/₈" across; press onto the hair. Slightly flatten a ⁵/₈" black ball and press into the center. Flatten terra cotta to ¹/₁₆" thick and cut a ¹/₈"x3" strip. Wrap it for a hat band, joining the ends in front. Cut a ¹/₄"x³/₈" rectangle and attach for the buckle; use a toothpick to imprint the inner lines. **Tie:** From the flattened black, cut two bow loops and two ¹/₈"x³/₄" strips for tails. Attach the tails below his chin, angling slightly apart. Fold the loops in half and attach them point to point over the top of the tails. Roll a ¹/₁₆" black ball and press into the center for a knot.

3 **Arms:** Roll two ³/₈"x1⁵/₈" white logs. Roll two ³/₈" beige balls and attach one to the lower end of each log. **Pumpkin:** Roll a ⁷/₈" orange ball; flatten slightly. Use a toothpick to draw the segment lines. Roll a ¹/₈" thick terra cotta rope, cut a ¹/₄" length and attach for the stem. Roll a ¹/₁₆"x2" green rope and attach near the stem, twisting and curling it into tendrils. Attach the pumpkin to his left hand.

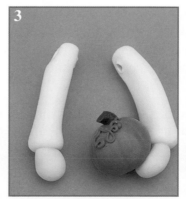 shoe shoe buckle hat buckle bow loop

4 **Legs:** Roll two ³/₈"x1⁵/₈" black logs. Roll two ⁹/₁₆" chocolate balls into ovals, slightly flatten one end of each, and attach the flattened ends to the bottoms of the legs. Imprint stitching lines around the soles. From flattened white, cut two ¹/₄"x3" strips. Wrap one around the bottom of each leg for a cuff, joining the ends in front. From flattened terra cotta, cut and imprint two ¹/₄" square buckles. Attach one to the front of each cuff. Pierce, bake and finish (see inside the back cover). Use the pen to draw his smile. Assemble.

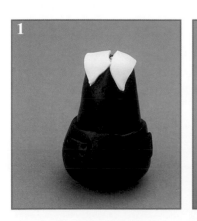
1

2

3

4

79

actual height 1¾"

The Last Straw
by Anita Behnen

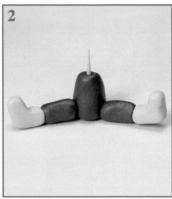

Sculpey®: black, ecru, green pearl, translucent
2½"x1" burgundy sunflower print fabriclay (see page 7)
½" tall wood bucket
2"x1½" piece of gray cardstock
1" long wired wood floral pick
1" wide straw hat
   18" long raffia strand
   small tuft of sheet moss
   red chalk
   2 size 12/0 black seed beads
black fine-tip permanent gel pen
1/16" hole punch
basic supplies (see inside the front cover)

vest

First, blend to make:
• green for clothing: 1" ball of green pearl + 1" black ball

1 **Body**: Shape a ¾" dark green ball into a ⅞" tall egg. Break a toothpick in half and insert the halves into the base of the egg, angled apart. Insert ⅓ of a toothpick into the body top so ½" extends.

2 **Legs**: Roll two ½" dark green balls into ¾" long logs and press onto the body base toothpicks. **Shoes**: Shape two ½" ecru balls into 1" long tapered logs. Bend each in half; pinch the bend to form the heel, then round the toe. Press the tapered ends onto the ends of the legs.

3 **Stitch marks**: Use a pin to draw a line down the front of the body, under the bottom and up the back. Repeat on each shoe. Draw a line along the inside and outside of each leg. Draw random short lines across these lines to resemble sloppy stitches. Make gather lines at the tops and bottoms of the legs and in the tops of the shoes.

4 **Vest**: Trace and cut out the pattern. Place on the clay side of the fabriclay and trace around it with the pin. Cut out. Wrap the vest around his body with the opening in the front.

5 **Arms**: Shape two ½" dark green balls into 1" long tapered logs. Bend at the elbows. Poke the stylus into the center of the wide end of each arm, rotating it to make a hole ¼" deep and ¼" wide. **Hands**: Shape two ¼" ecru balls into ½" long tapered logs. Pinch the wide ends flat. Press the tapered ends into the wrist holes. Use the stylus to poke three ¼" deep holes—one on the top and one on each side—in each wrist, angling them toward the elbow. Draw stitching lines and gathers as for the legs. Glue each inner arm as shown.

6 Apply glue to one side of the bucket and press it against the front of the scarecrow. Glue the insides of the hands onto the bucket as shown.

7 **Head**: Shape a ⅝" ecru ball into an egg. Press the head onto the body top toothpick. Attach a ⅛" ecru ball for the nose. Insert the seed beads for eyes.

8 Use the stylus to poke four ¼" deep holes in the bottom of the head extending up—one in front, one on each side and one in the back.

9 Use the needle to draw stitch marks (see page 80, step 3) along the sides of the face. Draw a smile and cross it with stitches. Blush the cheeks and nose with red chalk.

10 Glue the hat firmly onto his head. Cut a ⅛"x2" strip of fabriclay and glue it for the hatband.

11 Bake (see page 6); let cool. Cut a 1" long strand of raffia no more than ¼" wide (use your fingernail to split it if necessary). Fold in half and twist the fold to a point. Glue into one of the holes in the scarecrow's head or wrist. Repeat for the remaining holes. Let the glue dry, then use your fingernail to shred the raffia ends into thinner strips. Trim the ends if necessary.

12 **Sign**: Trim the corners of the cardstock to make an irregular board. Use the black pen to write "This Is The Last Straw" in the center. Punch two holes at the center top, ⅛" apart. Break off and discard the bottom ⅔ of the floral pick. Insert the wires through the holes, then wrap them securely around the top of the pick. Glue moss into the bucket. Glue the sign into the moss as shown in the large photo on page 80. Fold a 1½" strand of raffia and glue it beside the sign.

project stands 4¹/₄" tall

Autumn's Harvester
by Linda Welsh

Sculpey®: stone-look blue, pale peach, burgundy,
orange, green, tan, brown, yellow
1³/₄" tall terra cotta pot, pinking shears
⁵/₁₆" white button, dark brown acrylic paint
¹/₂" square fabric pieces: burgundy print, blue &
white checked
green excelsior, 28-gauge wire, two black seed beads
blond Lil Loopies hair, tan felt, soft cloth, tacky glue
clay cutters: ⁵/₁₆" flower, ³/₈" teardrop, ³/₁₆" circle
tan craft foam, black fine-tip permanent-ink pen
basic supplies (see inside the front cover)

1 Body: Roll a 1" blue ball into a cone; insert a toothpick to extend ¹/₂" from top and bottom. **Arms:** Roll two ⁵/₈" burgundy balls into ³/₄" long tapered logs; attach to shoulders. **Overalls:** Roll two ⁵/₁₆" blue balls into 1" long logs for straps. Flatten a ¹/₂"x³/₈" blue rectangle for a pocket. Press to his body as shown. Use the cutter to cut a ¹/₈" thick burgundy circle, indent the center with the pin head and poke two button holes. **Collar:** Flatten ¹/₂" peach ball to a ¹/₁₆" thick circle; use the pin to make crease lines on the top and press onto the neck pick, using your fingers to make ruffles.

2 Head: Press an ¹¹/₁₆" peach ball over the collar. Use the pin to indent neck lines. Press the seed beads for eyes; use the pin to make brows. Shape a ¹/₁₆" orange ball into a flattened triangle for a nose. Use the circle cutter to indent cheeks, use the pin to join the two in a smile and to make stitch lines. **Hat:** Flatten brown clay to ¹/₁₆" thick and cut a 1¹/₂" wide circle. Place on the back of his head for a brim. Flatten an ¹¹/₁₆" brown ball and press for the hat crown; fold the brim back over the crown.

3 Flowers: Flatten yellow clay to ¹/₁₆" and cut two flowers; repeat for green clay but cut five teardrops for leaves. Press the flowers and two leaves at the hat brim as shown adding an indented ¹/₈" orange ball to each flower center. **Pumpkins:** Roll two ⁹/₁₆" and one ¹¹/₁₆" orange balls. Use the pin to draw lines as shown. Press a leaf to each top and insert a ¹/₄" long toothpick; remove each toothpick and set aside. Indent a line along each leaf. Flatten a ¹/₁₆" and a ¹/₈" orange ball to a square. Repeat for green clay. Press one of each to each arm for patches and indent stitch marks as shown. Roll two ⁷/₁₆" tan balls for hands.

4 Use the hair to make three pom poms (see page 63) of six loops each. Use the wire ends to poke holes in his head for placement then set aside. Bake (see page 6) all pieces; reinsert the pumpkin stems. Cut two ³/₄" felt circles; cut fringes ¹/₈" in from the edge around them. Glue the felt to the arm ends and the hands to the felt. Embellish the pot as shown above and stuff it with grass, glue the Scarecrow and pumpkins into it. Antique the project then seal. Use the craft foam, pen and pinking shears to make the sign, glue it to a notched toothpick and glue it as shown. Glue and insert his hair.

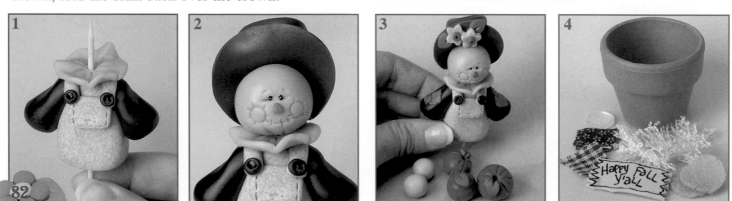

Crow on Pumpkins

by Linda Welsh

Sculpey®: orange, green, black
2 black seed beads
two 2¹/₂" lengths of 24-gauge black wire
brown acrylic paint
clay cutters: ³/₈" flower, ⁷/₁₆" and ³/₈" teardrops
basic supplies (see inside the front cover)

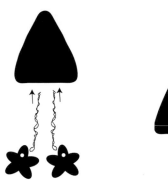

project is 2¹/₄" tall.

1 Pumpkins: Roll two ⁵/₈" and one ⁷/₈" orange balls. Use the pin to indent lines in each and place as shown. Roll green clay to ¹/₈" thick; cut 4 small and 2 large teardrops for leaves. Indent each leaf and press to each pumpkin top angled outward. Use the paintbrush and brown paint to paint two ¹/₂" toothpicks and insert one to extend from each small pumpkin.

2 *For the Crow...* Body: Shape an ¹¹/₁₆" black ball into a rounded triangle. **Feet:** Roll black clay ¹/₈" thick and cut two flowers. Poke a hole through each and bake (see page 6) for 10 minutes. Set aside for step 4. **Wings:** Shape two ³/₈" black balls into ¹/₂" long teardrops; press a wing to each shoulder. Press his body onto the large pumpkin and insert a toothpick through his body and into the pumpkin. Trim it to extend ¹/₄" from his neck. Insert half a toothpick into the side of each small pumpkin and press into the large pumpkin to position them as shown.

3 Head: Shape a ¹/₂" black ball into a rounded triangle; use your fingers to taper the tip and curl it over a toothpick for the hair flip. Press his head onto his neck. Press the seed beads for eyes and shape a ¹/₈" orange ball into a triangle for his beak.

4 Remove the pumpkin stems. Thread a 2¹/₂" wire length through a foot hole so the foot is in the wire center. Fold the wire ends together and twist as shown. Repeat for the other foot. Insert the legs into the body front ¹/₈" apart. Bake then replace the pumpkin stems when cool. Seal (see page 7).

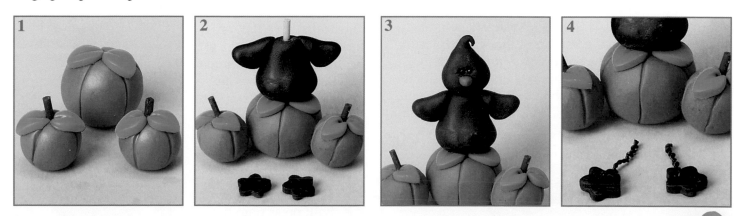

project sits 3" tall

Snow Cookies
by Linda Welsh

*Sculpey®: white, red,
    fluorescent green, brown,
    orange*
*clay cutters: ³/₈" and ³/₁₆"
    hearts*
*⁵/₁₆" long holly leaf punch
    (optional), or use the
    pattern below*
coffee stirrer
two black seed beads
white craft foam
pinking shears
opalescent glitter
pink chalk, small paintbrush
*black fine-tip permanent-ink
    pen*
*basic supplies (see inside the
    front cover)*

First, blend to make:
• pink: 1¹/₈" ball of white + ¹¹/₁₆" ball of red
• light pink: ³/₄" ball of white + ⁵/₁₆" ball of pink

1 Holly leaves: Flatten green clay to ¹/₃₂" thick; bake for 1 minute. Insert the clay as if it were paper into the punch and punch four holly leaves. Bake for 10 minutes. Let cool and set aside for steps 3 and 4. **Shoes:** Use the shoe pattern to shape a ⁵/₈" pink ball. Use a ³/₈" light pink ball to make the sole. Shape a ⁵/₁₆" pink ball into a square. Flatten a ¹/₄" light pink ball, shape into a square and press to the bottom of the square piece. Press the square to the narrow end of the shoe for a heel. Flatten a ⁵/₈"x³/₈" white oval and press for a sock, poking pin holes as shown. Roll a ¹/₈"x1" pink log; wrap for a strap. Flatten two ¹/₈" light pink balls and press on each side for clasps. Repeat to make another shoe.

2 Body: Shape a 1¹/₄" white ball into a cone. Flatten two ¹/₂" white balls and press onto lower sides for legs; press a shoe onto each leg. Shape two ³/₄" white balls into a 1¹/₂" long tapered logs; press a narrow end to each shoulder for arms and curve as shown. **Collar:** Flatten pink to ¹/₁₆" thick and cut a 1¹/₈" circle and cut in half. Scallop (see page 7) the round edges of each and indent each scallop with the coffee stirrer. Use the pin to make tri-dots randomly around the collar; place them over her shoulders and insert a toothpick to extend ¹/₂". Flatten green clay to ³/₈"; use the ⁵/₈" heart cutter to cut two hearts. Place them, points together for a bow. Cut and place two ³/₄"x¹/₄" bow tails. Use the pin to press a ¹/₈" green ball to the bow center, and to make a crease line in each heart center.

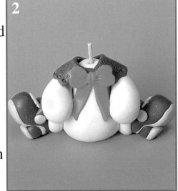

3 Head: Roll a 1" white ball; press onto the toothpick. Press the seed beads for eyes; roll a 1/8" orange ball and press for her nose. Press the small heart to each cheek to imprint then use the pin to draw her brows and smile. Use the paintbrush and chalk to blush her cheeks. **Hat:** Cut a 2" circle, scallop the edges and imprint each with the coffee stirrer. Turn so the stamped design is down and place it on her head using your fingers to fold in ruffles. Shape a 3/4" pink ball into a rounded square and press to her head for a hat crown. Flatten and cut a 3/16"x2 1/4" white strip and wrap for a hat band. Press three holly leaves and three 1/8" pink balls as shown; press a 1/16" white ball to each holly berry and poke with a toothpick to indent.

4 **Basket:** Flatten a 3/4" brown ball to 1/2" thick; make cross-hatch lines with the pin for wicker. Flatten light pink clay to 1/16" thick and cut a 1 1/2" wide circle. Cut it in half, elongate one

piece into a flat rounded triangle. Scallop the edges and drape over the basket. Twist two 1/8"x3" long brown logs together, trim to 2" and attach as shown for a handle. Roll many 1/8" white balls and stack into the basket for cookies. Make 3 holly berries as for her hat and place with a leaf as shown. Place the basket between her legs as shown. Bake (see inside the back cover). Use the craft foam pen and pinking shears to make the sign. Glue the sign as shown. Sprinkle with glitter and seal (see page 7).

Gingerbread Ornament
by Linda Welsh

Sculpey®: brown
15" strip of 1/2" wide burgundy print fabric
18" length of 22-gauge wire
7" length of white baby rickrack
3/16" heart clay cutter
jewelry glue (such as E6000™ or Goop®)
basic supplies (see inside the front cover)

1 **Body:** Shape a 1 1/8" ball into a cone and flatten slightly. Use the knife to make a 3/8" cut up the bottom center; shape each side as shown in the photo. Roll two 5/8" balls into 1 1/8" long tapered logs; press a narrow end to each shoulder for arms. Use a toothpick to push a hole into each hand; push a toothpick into his neck to extend 1/2". Press a 3/4" ball onto the toothpick. Press the seed beads in for eyes, a 1/16" ball for a nose and use the pin to make lashes.

ornament is 3 3/4" tall with wire

2 **Accents:** Use the heart cutter to imprint two hearts down the body center and one on each cheek; use the pin to make stitch marks and the paintbrush and chalk to blush each heart. Bake (see page 6) let it cool and seal (see page 7). Coil the wire around the paintbrush handle; remove it, stretch it a bit and insert one end into each hand hole. Turn up the ends to secure. Cut a 6" fabric length and make a bow to glue below his chin. Tie the remaining fabric in a bow around the wire. Cut two 1 1/2" lengths of rickrack; glue around each wrist. Cut and glue a 2" length for a head band and wrap the remaining rickrack around his legs as shown.

85

Snow Scene
by Linda Welsh

Sculpey®: yellow, red, green, brown, white, blue, orange
two black seed beads
1" length of 24-gauge black wire
8" length of 28-gauge silver wire
white cardstock
jewelry glue (such as E6000™ or Goop®)
opalescent glitter
faux snow texture
1/2" wide snowflake punch (optional), or use the pattern below
basic supplies (see inside the front cover)

Snow Scene is 3¼" tall

Black symbolizes white clay

1 **Jellyroll candy:** Flatten red and white clay to ¹/₁₆" thick. Cut a 1"x2" piece of each color. For the red candies, lay the red on the white, roll it as shown in the diagram then roll the log until it s about 5" long. Bake it (see page 6) for 5 minutes and slice seven to nine ¹/₈" pieces. Repeat for the yellow and green candies; set aside for step 4. **Snowflakes:** Punch four snowflakes from white cardstock, then glue them to the wire; set aside for step 6. **Base:** Flatten a 1¹/₈" white ball in the palm of your hand until it s 2" around; an uneven top is okay and adds to the "snowy hill" appearance.

2 **For the Snowman…**
Body: Roll an ¹¹/₁₆", ⁹/₁₆" and a ⁷/₁₆" white ball. Stack them as listed on the right side of the snowy hill. **Buttons:** Flatten a red, yellow, green and blue ¹/₁₆" ball and press to his front as shown. Poke each twice with the pin point for button holes. **Arms:** Insert the black wire through his middle below the scarf to extend ¹/₄" from each side. **Ear Muffs:** Roll a ¹/₁₆"x¹/₂" blue log; flatten two ³/₁₆" blue balls and press to his head as shown. **Face:** Press the seed beads in his face for eyes, shape a ¹/₁₆" orange ball into a triangle and press for a nose and use the pin to poke four holes in a curve below his nose for a smile.

3 **Scarf:** Flatten blue and white clay to 1"x3½"x¹⁄₃₂" each, lay the blue on the white, cut it lengthwise into quarters and stack them alternating colors. Cut a ¼"x4" strip and wrap around his neck for a scarf, arranging the ends as shown. Trim any excess.

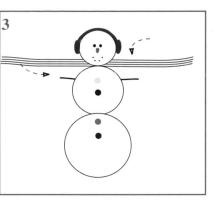

4 **Birdhouse:** Shape a ⅞" brown ball into a rounded triangle; tap the sides with your finger to square them slightly. Use the pin to indent hatch marks on the walls for wood. Roll a ⅛"x3" red log; wrap it around the house foundation and trim the excess. Flatten and cut a ³⁄₁₆"x¼" white door and press to the house front; use the pin to indent stitching around the door and to make a doorknob. Insert a ½" toothpick above the door as shown then remove it until step 6. Shape a ⅜" brown ball to a ¼" square; shave off one side so it will sit as a chimney on the roof—don t apply it until step 6. Insert a toothpick into the underside of the house for a post, then into the snowy hill left of the snowman; remove the toothpick and set the house aside until step 6.

5 **Candycanes:** Roll a red ⅛"x4" log; repeat with white clay. Lie the logs together and twist them; cut them in half and shape each into a cane. Insert half of a toothpick into the straight ends of each leaving ¼" exposed. Insert it into the snowy hill angled as shown in front of where the house will stand.

6 **Tree:** Shape a ½", ⁷⁄₁₆" and a ⅜" green ball into triangles. Stack them as listed flattening the tips of the lower two as necessary. Press the tree to the left side of the snowy hill as shown. **Snowballs:** Roll twenty-three ³⁄₁₆"–¼" white balls. Place four in a pyramid on the right of the snowman, four in a square left of the tree and three in a pile at the forefront of the snowy hill. Pile the remaining snowballs around the tree and especially around the candy canes and house post hole to help support them.

7 Bake the snowy hill, house and candies. After cooling, glue and insert the house post. Reinsert the bird perch as shown. Glue the candies on the roof and glue the chimney to the roof as shown. Wad up ¼" of each wire end into a ball shape for stability. Glue one behind the snowman and the other behind the tree forming an arch. Use a toothpick to dab a bit of faux snow to the chimney, snowman s head, the tree and a few of the snowballs. Sprinkle the entire project with glitter for glistening snow.

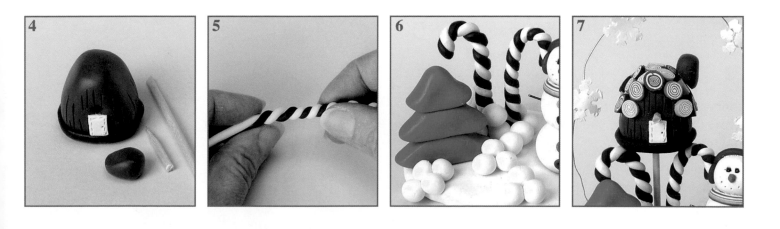

actual height 1¾"

Penguin & Pal
by Anita Behnen

Sculpey®: black, white, cadmium yellow, red pearl
¼"x3" strip of green star/dot fabric
¼"x3" strip of red star/dot fabric
4 size 12/0 black seed beads
½ tsp. of white embossing powder
red chalk, small paintbrush
³⁄₁₆" star clay cutter (or use this pattern)
basic supplies (see inside the front cover)

First, set aside a pinch of embossing powder for step 7. To make speckled red: knead the remaining emobssing powerd + 1" ball of red pearl clay.

1 **Penguin**: Shape a ¾" black ball into an egg. Break a toothpick into thirds. Insert ⅓ into the top so that ¼" extends. Insert two into the lower sides as shown. Shape a ¼" white ball into an egg and flatten to ¹⁄₁₆" thick. Press it onto the body front, then smooth the edges down so the tummy appears continuous with the black sides.

2 **Boots:** Roll two ⅝" yellow balls into 1" long tapered logs. Bend each in half; pinch the bend to form the heel, then round the toe. Press the tapered ends onto the lower toothpicks. Use the pin to draw lines dividing the heels from the soles and the soles from the shoe tops.

3 **Wings:** Roll two ½" balls of black clay into tapered logs. Flatten slightly, then pinch the ends to form a diamonds. Bend each wing slightly inward. Press the sides to the shoulders with the elbows resting on the boots.

4 **Head:** Roll a ⅝" black ball into an egg. Press the head onto the body top toothpick. **Eyes:** Flatten a ⅛" white ball into a triangle and press onto the center front of the head, wide end down. Use the pin to draw a line down the center. Insert two seed beads as shown.

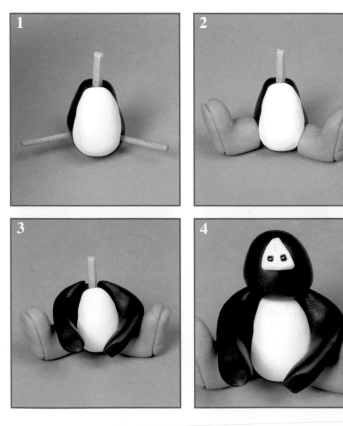

5 **Beak:** Shape a $3/16"$ yellow ball into a cone and press onto the face, slightly overlapping the eyes. Use the pin to poke two nostril holes and draw a smile line around the beak.

6 **Hat:** Shape a $7/8"$ speckled red ball into a $1\frac{1}{2}"$ tall cone. Use the stylus to start a hole in the wide end, then press in with your thumb, turning the cone as you pinch the edge until the brim is $1\frac{1}{8}"$ wide and the center is hollowed to $3/4"$ deep. Place the hat on the penguin's head.

7 Slightly flatten the tail of the hat. Twist it 2–3 times, then bend the tip toward the front of the hat. Cut three stars from the red fabric and three more from the green fabric. Glue a red and green star side by side on the right front of the hat. Repeat on the left back and the right back. Use the pin to draw stitches around each patch. Flatten a $1/4"$ white ball to $1/16"$ thick and use the clay cutter to cut a star. Press the star onto the hat tip. Use your forefinger to apply white embossing powder to the front edge of the hat.

8 **Bear**: Roll a $1/2"$ white ball into an egg. **Legs:** Roll two $3/8"$ balls of white clay into $3/4"$ long tapered logs. Bend each into an L and round the toe. Press the tapered ends onto the bottom sides of the body, crossing the toes as shown. **Arms:** Roll two $5/16"$ white balls into $1/2"$ long tapered logs and bend the elbows. Attach one to each shoulder.

9 **Head:** Shape a $3/8"$ white ball into an egg and attach to the body top. Shape a $1/16"$ black ball into an oval and attach $3/4$ of the way down the head for a nose. Insert two seed beads for eyes. **Ears:** Press a $1/8"$ white ball onto each side of the head top. Use the stylus to indent the center fronts.

10 Use the pin to draw a vertical line below the nose. Draw a smile below the line. Flatten a $1/8"$ red ball and pinch one side to a point. Use the side of the pin to indent the top, forming a heart. Attach the heart to the center of his chest. Blush his cheeks and the top of his head.

11 Press the bear into the angle of the penguin's left leg and body. Curve the penguin's left arm down behind the bear's left shoulder. Press the penguin's right hand against the bear's right arm.

(Refer to the large photo on page 88.) Bake (see page 6). Keep an eye on them during baking; if the bear seems to be browning, turn the oven temperature down 15°–20° to finish baking. Let cool. Tie the remaining green fabric around the penguin's neck and the remaining red fabric around the bear's neck as shown in the large photo on page 88.

Chill Out by Shelly Comiskey

actual height 3⅜"

*Sculpey®: sweet potato, white, blue pearl
¾" long finger cut from a blue knit cotton glove
about a hundred 3x5mm clear acrylic pellets
½"x6" strip of light blue polka-dot fabric
2" wide metal washtub
two 1½" long twigs
2 size 15/0 black seed beads
¾"x½" piece of light blue cardstock
2" of 26-gauge black wire
white snow-texture paint
white flocking kit
watercolor pens: blue, black
3/16" heart clay cutter (or use the pattern above)
chalk: pink, light blue
E-6000™ glue
1/16" hole punch
basic supplies (see inside the front cover)*

First, blend to make:
• light blue: ½" ball of blue pearl + ⅞" ball of white

1 Fill the washtub ⅔ full of scrap or white clay. Shape a 1½" white ball into a pear. Press the wide end into the washtub. Push a toothpick through the body into the washtub clay, leaving ¼" extending at the neck. Roll a 1⅛" white ball and press onto the neck. Insert a twig into each side of the body so 1" extends. Flatten light blue to 1/16" thick and use the cutter to cut two hearts. Press onto the body front. Use the pin to poke two holes in each heart and draw a thin line between the holes.

2 Face: Roll a ¼" sweet potato ball into a ½" long cone. Twist slightly and press onto the face as shown. Use the pin to draw carroty lines and a crooked smile. Insert the seed beads for eyes. Draw a short, angled eyebrow above each eye. Blush the cheeks with pink chalk; shade the eyes and mouth with blue. Remove the twig arms. Bake (see page 6); let cool.

3 Sign: Trace and cut out the oval pattern. Lay on the cardstock and trace with the black pen. Cut just outside the black line. Write "Chill Out!" in the center. Draw a heart at the bottom and color it blue. Make blue squiqqles along the letters and in the empty areas. Make clusters of three black dots throughout. Apply snow paint as shown; let dry. Punch two holes ½" apart at the top. Bend the wire into a curve and insert the ends through the holes. Bend them up in back.

4 Follow the instructions with the flocking kit to paint the snowman white and flock him. Fill the bottom of the washtub with E-6000™. Sprinkle acrylic pellets thickly onto the glue. Let the flocking and glue set for couple of hours. Follow page 37, step 10 to make the cap. Glue onto the head as shown in the large photo above. Glue the arms back into their holes. Tie the fabric around his neck for a scarf. Apply snow paint randomly to the hat, arms, "ice" and washtub. Hang the sign on his hand and secure with a dab of glue.

Think Snow by Shelly Comiskey

Sculpey®: white, ecru, sweet potato
white cotton knit child s glove, hot coffee or tea
12" square of aluminum foil
½"x⅞" piece of tan cardstock
fine-tip permanent gel pens: black, white
1½" Styrofoam® ball   *talcum powder*
decorative snowflakes
white snow-texture paint
chalk: pink, light blue
³⁄₁₆" heart clay cutter (or
*   use the pattern above)*
2 size 15/0 black seed
*   beads*
needle
6" of metallic gold thread
basic supplies (see inside
*   the front cover)*

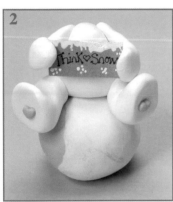

actual height 3½" excluding hanger

First, roll a 1½" ball of scrap clay and flatten the bottom so it will sit. Bake (see page 6); let cool. Dust with talcum. This "working base" will be replaced with the foam ball after baking. Dye the glove by soaking it in hot coffee or tea for 20 minutes; let dry.

1 **Sign**: Use the black pen to write "Think Snow" in the center of the cardstock. Use the white pen to drizzle snow along the top and make clusters of five dots to represent snowflakes. Let dry.

2 **Body**: Roll a ⅞" white ball into a pear. Press onto the top of the scrap base. **Arms**: Roll two ½" white balls into 1" long tapered logs. Attach the small ends to the shoulders. Place the sign between the hands and gently pinch the hands to hold it. **Legs**: Roll two white ⅝" white balls into ⅞" long tapered logs. Use your thumb to flatten the wide end of each and push up a foot. Attach the small ends to the body. Curve the legs downward over the powdered base as shown. Flatten ecru to ¹⁄₁₆" thick and cut two ³⁄₁₆" hearts. Press one onto the bottom of each foot.

3 **Head**: Roll a ¾" white ball and attach to the body top. Roll a ³⁄₁₆" sweet potato ball into an oval and attach for the nose. Insert the seed beads for eyes. Use the pin to draw eyelashes and a smile. Blush the cheeks with pink chalk and shade the eyes with blue. Remove the sign. Remove the snowman from the ball and use a toothpick to make a hole in his base, then replace him. Bake; let cool.

4 **Snowball**: Insert a toothpick into the foam ball for a handle. Brush glue all over the ball, then sprinkle liberally with snow; let dry.

(Refer to the large photo.) Crumple the foil into a log, then shape it into a donut to support the snowball. Glue the snowman onto the toothpick and let the glue dry. Glue the sign into his hands. Follow page 37, step 10 to make the cap. Glue it onto his head. Cut a ½"x4" strip from another part of the glove and tie it around his neck for a scarf. Dab snow paint onto the hat and his toes. Sew the gold thread through the hat top and knot the ends for a hanger.

Arctic Pile
by Shelly Comiskey

actual height 3"

Sculpey®: white, black, orange
4 black glass seed beads
2 blue glass seed beads
basic supplies (see inside the front cover)

First, blend to make:
• gray: 1" white ball + ⅝" black ball

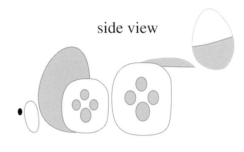

side view

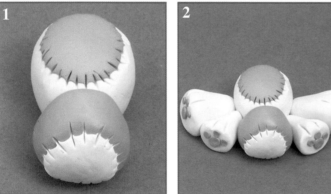

1 Husky—Body: Shape a 1¼" white ball into an egg. Lay on its side and press the bottom flat. Flatten a ³/₈" gray ball to ¹/₁₆" thick. Press into the center top of the body. **Head:** Shape a ⁷/₈" gray ball into a rounded triangle. Shape a ³/₈" white ball into a rounded triangle. Flatten to ¹/₁₆" thick. Press into the center of the head. Attach to the narrow end of the body, making sure the chin touches the table. Use the pin to imprint fur lines along the outer edges of the face and body top.

2 Legs: Shape two ⁵/₈" white balls and two ¹³/₁₆" white balls into tapered logs. Indent the wide end of each with your thumb. Attach the small ends to the body, behind the head as shown. **Pads:** Flatten twelve ¹/₁₆" gray balls. Attach three to the end of each leg in a triangle. Shape four ¹/₈" gray balls into ovals and flatten. Attach one under each triangle as shown. Use the pin to make two toe lines in the top of each leg.

3 Tail: Roll an ¹¹/₁₆" gray ball into a ³/₄" long tapered log. Roll an ¹¹/₁₆" white ball into a ³/₄" long tapered log. Press the wide ends of the logs together. Roll smooth and shape each end to a point. Use the pin to imprint fur lines between the colors. Gently bend and press to the back of the body as shown.

4 Face: Flatten two ³/₁₆" gray balls into rounded triangles. Indent the centers with the round end of the pin and press together in the center top of the

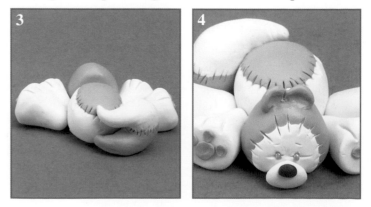

92

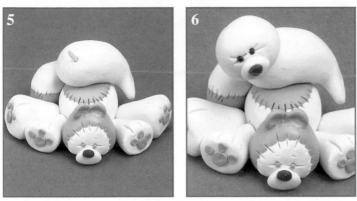

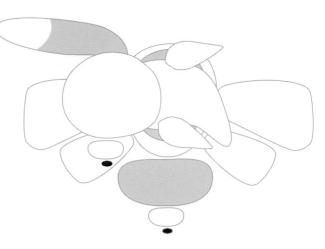

top view

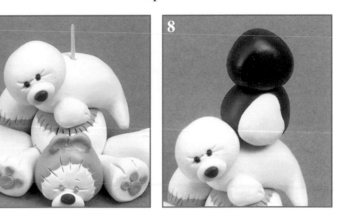

head. Shape a 5/16" white ball into a rounded triangle and press onto the lower face for the muzzle, with the wide end touching the table. Shape a 1/8" black ball into an oval and attach for the nose. Insert two blue seed beads (see page 7) above the muzzle for eyes. Use the pin to draw an eyebrow above each eye.

5 **Seal—Body:** Shape a 1" white ball into a 1 1/2" long teardrop. Press the wide end onto the top of the husky s body, gently curving the narrow end forward and down, flattening it as shown. Insert a 1/2" toothpick into the neck front, extending 1/4", and angled slightly forward.

6 **Head:** Slightly flatten a 7/8" white ball. Push onto the toothpick. Shape a 1/4"white ball into a rounded triangle and press onto the bottom of the face. Shape a 1/8" black ball into a rounded triangle and attach for the nose. Insert two black beads above the muzzle for eyes. Use the pin to draw two eyelashes beside each eye.

7 **Flippers:** Shape two 7/16" white balls into teardrops. Press one onto each shoulder, resting on the husky s body and pointing toward the tail. Use the pin to indent marks at the end of the flippers and tail. Insert a toothpick into the top of the seal s body, through the husky s body, leaving 1/2" extending upward.

8 **Penguin—Body:** Shape a 7/8" black ball into an egg. Shape a 7/16" white ball into a teardrop, indenting the top right side, and flatten to 1/8" thick. Attach to the body front. Press the wide end onto the toothpick to rest on the seal, angled slightly right. Attach a 13/16" black rounded triangle to the top of the body for a head.

9 **Wings:** Shape two 3/8" black balls into teardrops. Place one on each side of the body. Shape two 3/16" orange balls into flat triangles. Attach them for feet as shown. **Face:** Shape a 3/16" orange ball into a cone and press onto the center of the face. Insert two black beads for eyes above the beak. Roll a 3/16" black ball into a 1/2" long log. Cut into two unequal lengths and attach side by side to the top of the head, curving as shown. Bake (page 6).

93

Kristofer Klaus

by Judy Ferrill

Sculpey®: red, white, beige, green, black
1¹/₂" tall Christmas tree
acrylic paint: black, white
#0 liner paintbrush
garlic press or Kemper Klaygun
#3 wide white perle cotton or heavy white carpet thread
four ¹/₄" wide white buttons with 2 holes
black permanent marking pen
basic supplies (see inside the front cover)

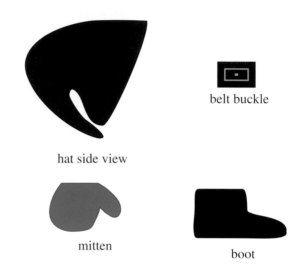

hat side view

belt buckle

mitten

boot

1 Body: Shape a 1¹/₈" red ball into a 1³/₈" tall cone. Roll a ³/₄" beige ball and attach (see page 7) for his head. Attach a ¹/₈" beige ball for his nose. Shape a 1" red ball into a cone, indent the flat end and attach for his hat. Flatten white to ¹/₈" thick and cut a ¹/₄"x4" strip. Wrap around the body bottom, joining and smoothing the ends. Repeat for the hat brim. Repeat with black for the belt. Cut a ¹/₄"x³/₈" black square, imprint as shown and attach for the buckle. Pull the hat tip down and attach it to his back just above the belt.

2 Make the white hair, attaching it over the front edge of the hat brim overlapping the face. Squeeze out ¹/₂"–³/₄" lengths for the beard; attach as shown.

3 Arms: Roll two ³/₈"x1¹/₂" red logs. Shape two ¹/₂" green balls to match the mitten pattern and attach to the bottoms of the arms. Cut two ¹/₄"x2" strips of flattened white and attach for the cuff trim, joining and smoothing the ends.

4 Legs: Roll two ³/₈"x1³/₄" red logs. Shape two ⁵/₈" black balls to match the boot pattern and attach to the leg bottoms. Add cuff trim as for the arms. Pierce, bake, finish and assemble (see inside the back cover). Lacquer the belt and boots. Glue the tree into his left hand as shown in the large photo.

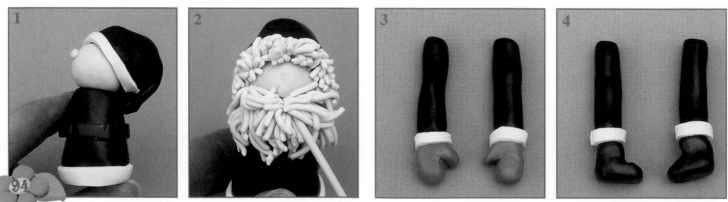

Frau Klaus by Judy Ferrill

Sculpey®: white red, beige, black, gray
heart clay cutters: ³/₁₆", ¹/₄" (or use the patterns)
1" wide gold glasses (or shape from 22-gauge gold
  wire as on page 47, step 4)
¹/₂" square gold wrapped miniature gift
acrylic paint: black, white
#0 liner paintbrush
garlic press or Kemper Klaygun
#3 wide white perle cotton or heavy white carpet thread
four ¹/₄" wide white buttons with 2 holes
black permanent marking pen
basic supplies (see inside the front cover)

First, blend to make:
• gray: 1" white ball + ⅝" black ball.

heart   hand   shoe

1 **Body:** Shape a 1¹/₈" red ball into a 1³/₄" tall cone.
Apron: Flatten white to ¹/₁₆" and cut a 3¹/₄"x1¹/₈"
piece. Scallop (see page 7) the lower edge and both
short edges. Cut out a ¹/₄" heart from the lower right
center. Wrap around the body with the scallops even
with the bottom edge. Cut two ¹/₄"x³/₈" white pockets
and attach on the right side. Use the tip of a toothpick
to imprint stitches around the pockets and gather lines
at the apron top. Cut two ¹/₈"x2" white strips and
attach as shown for suspenders. Flatten red to ¹/₁₆",
cut four ³/₁₆" hearts and attach for front and back
suspender buttons. Use the toothpick to imprint button
holes.

2 **Head:** Roll a ⁷/₈" beige ball and attach. Roll a
¹/₁₆" beige ball for her nose. Make gray hair.
Cap: Use the flattened white, cut a ³/₄" circle and
attach to the top of her head.

3 From the flattened red, cut a ¹/₄"x4" strip. Attach
it around the white circle, using the side of a
toothpick to gently gather it into upright ruffles.

Arms: Roll two ³/₈"x1³/₈" red logs, shaping them
slightly larger at the lower end. Flatten two ³/₈" beige
balls and shape to match the hand pattern. Attach one
at the bottom of each arm.

4 **Legs:** Shape two ¹/₂" red balls into ⁵/₈" tall cones.
Roll two ¹/₄"x1" beige logs and attach one to the
flat end of each cone. From the flattened white cut two
³/₁₆"x2" strips. Scallop the top edges and wrap around
the leg bottoms for socks. **Shoes:** Roll two ⁹/₁₆" black
balls into ovals, slightly flatten one end of each and
attach the flattened ends at the bottoms of the legs.
Pierce, bake and finish (see inside the back cover);
use the black pen to add a smile. Assemble the pieces.
Glue the glasses onto her face and the gift into her
right hand. Seal the shoes.

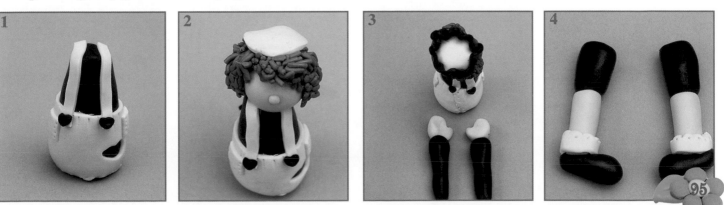

95

actual height 1⅝"

Gingerbread Boy
by Shelly Comiskey

Sculpey®: raw sienna, white, cadmium red, ecru
2 size 15/0 black seed beads
snow-textured paint
heart clay cutters: ³⁄₁₆", ⁵⁄₁₆" or use the patterns
embroidery floss: red, white
3" long green miniature artificial pine garland
white dimensional paint
embossing powders: blue, red
red chalk, small paintbrush
basic supplies (see inside the front cover)

1 Body: Shape a ¾" sienna ball into a pear. **Legs:** Shape two ¾" sienna balls into tapered logs. Use your thumb to press the wide end of each upward, forming a foot. Attach a leg to each side of the body as shown.

2 Arms: Roll two ⅝" sienna balls into tapered logs. Slightly flatten each wide end to form hands. Attach the points to the body top and curve the arms so the palms turn upward. **Head:** Shape a ⅝" sienna ball into a rounded triangle and attach to the top of the body. Insert seed beads for the eyes. Use the pin to draw the mouth, eyebrows and eyelashes. Attach a ³⁄₁₆" red ball for the nose. Blush the cheeks.

3 Roll a ½" ball of white into a ¹⁄₁₆" thick snake. Cut two 2" lengths and wrap one around the base of each foot. Cut a 1½" length to wrap around each wrist. Cut two ½" lengths, form each into a loop and attach, points together, to the top of his head. Flatten red clay to ¹⁄₁₆" thick and use the heart cutter to cut three hearts. Press one onto the bottom of each foot and one onto his left rump. Press two ⅛" red balls onto his tummy for buttons.

4 Candy canes: Roll a ¼" red ball into a ¹⁄₁₆" thick snake; repeat with white. Twist together and roll to smooth and reduce to ¹⁄₁₆" thick. Cut two ⅞" lengths and curve each into a candy cane. **Berries:** Roll six ¹⁄₁₆" red balls and attach in groups of three. **Cookie:** Flatten ecru to ⅛" thick and cut a ⁵⁄₁₆" heart. Bake (see page 6) the figure, cookie, berry clusters and candy canes. Let cool.

(Refer to the large photo.) Squeeze dimensional paint "frosting" onto the cookie, then use a toothpick to make a tiny white dot on each of the gingerbread boy s cheek. Lightly sprinkle the cookie with blue and red embossing powders. Drape the garland over his hands. Brush snow onto the garland; let dry. Glue the cookie, candy canes and berries as shown. Cut a 9" length each of red and white floss. Separate one strand of red and set aside. Hold the remaining red together with the white, wrap around his neck and tie in a shoestring bow at the side back, making ½" loops and ½" tails. Tie two shoestring bows in the single strand, each with ¼" loops and ¼" tails (it s easier to tie the bows, then cut them off the strand). Glue one to each side of the garland over the hands.

Reindeer & Elf Ornaments

by Shohreh Dolkhani

for each ornament:
basic supplies (see inside the front cover)
*1³/4" round glass Christmas ball, any color
aluminum foil
pink powder blush
acrylic paints: light blue, black, white
#0 liner paintbrush
black fine tip permant marker pen
for the reindeer:
Sculpey®: tan, dark rose, yellow
two 1" long Y-shaped twigs
for the elf:
Sculpey®: pale peach, red, green, white
* Check that the glass is heat-resistant and won't bleed color.
  Most glass balls can handle the baking required for this
  project. To be sure, test bake a single ball.

elf hat

reindeer 2¾" tall,
excluding antlers;
elf 3¼" tall

1 Separate the glass ball from the metal hanger. Save the wire part of the hanger. Use foil to make a 1¹/8" wide donut; prop the ball on it for assembly and baking. **Reindeer:** Shape a ³/4" tan ball into a rounded triangle. Press onto the top of the ball. Shape a ³/16" rose ball into a rounded triangle and attach for a nose. Use the pin to draw a vertical mouth below the nose. Shape two ⁵/16" tan balls into teardrops. Attach for ears. Use a toothpick to imprint a crease in each. Blush the cheeks and ears.

2 *Collar:* Flatten yellow to ¹/16" thick and cut a ³/8"x2" strip. Wrap around his neck. *Bow:* Cut three ¹/4"x1¹/4" strips. Trim the lower ends of two in inverted "V"'s. Attach the tops to the left collar. Fold the ends of the last strip to the center. Pinch the center and press onto the collar. *Antlers:* Push the twigs into his head between his ears. Use the pin to make three dots in each cheek.

3 **Elf:** Shape a 1" peach ball into a rounded triangle. Press onto the top of the ball. *Nose:* Shape a ¹/4" peach ball into an oval. Attach to his face. *Hat:* Roll a 1¹/8" green ball to ³/32" thick and cut out the hat pattern above. Wrap the hat around the top edge of his head, seam in the back. Roll red clay to ¹/16" thick. Cut a ¹/4"x2¹/2"

red strip and wrap around the lower edge. *Ears:* Shape two ⁷/16" peach balls into ovals; pull the tops into rounded points. Use the ball of a pin to push onto the sides of the head, extending over the hatband.

elf scarf

4 Bend the hat tip down as shown. Use the pin head to hollow out the center of a ⁵/16" red ball and attach over the hat tip. *Scarf:* Cut a ¹/2"x4¹/2" strip from the flattened red clay and trim to match the pattern. Wrap around his neck. Use the knife to imprint fringe. *Eyebrows:* Shape two ¹/8" white balls into ovals and attach to the bottom front of the hatband. Blush the cheeks, nose and ears.

For each ornament: Twist the wire ends of the hanger to make a loop. Push the twisted ends into the ornament top so that only the loop extends. Bake (see page 6). Paint the eyes (see page 7). Use a toothpick to make white dip dots (see inside the back cover) in groups of three on each ball. Let dry.

97

Santa & Reindeer
by Shelly Comiskey

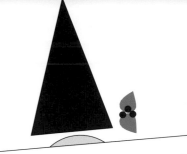

Sculpey®: red, white, green, brown, dark brown, tan, black, pink, yellow, pale peach
2 black glass seed beads
basic supplies (see inside the front cover)

actual height 3½"

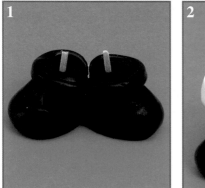

1 **Santa—Boots:** Use the pattern to shape two ¹³/₁₆" black balls into boots. Attach them side by side, toes outward as shown. Push a ½" long toothpick into the center top of each boot, angled slightly inward. Roll a ⁷/₁₆" black ball into a 2½" long log. Flatten to ³/₁₆" wide. Start at the center back and wrap around the boots for cuffs. Trim off any extra clay. Use the pin to press in the center front as shown.

2 **Body:** Shape a 1¼" red ball into an egg. Press the wide end onto the toothpicks at the top of the boots. **Coat Trim:** Roll a ⁵/₈" white ball into a 5" long log. Flatten to ¼" wide. Start at the center back and wrap around the lower body. Trim off any extra clay. **Belt:** Roll a ⁹/₁₆" black ball into a 4" long log. Flatten to ⅛" wide. Start at the center back and wrap around the middle body. Trim off any extra clay. Use the round end of the pin to press a ¼" yellow ball into the belt for the buckle.

3 **Arms:** Shape two ⁵/₈" red balls into tapered logs. Flatten a ⁷/₁₆" white ball to ½" wide and press to the wide end of each arm. Attach a ³/₈" green ball to each cuff. Attach an arm on each side of the body as shown, with the small ends at the shoulders. Push a ½" long toothpick into the center top of the body.

4 **Head:** Press the center of a $^7/8$" peach ball onto the toothpick at the top of the body. Shape a $1^1/16$" white ball into a $^3/8$" thick log. Taper at both ends and wrap around the chin, starting at the center back of the head, for the beard. Flatten a $^3/8$" white ball into an oval and press onto the back of the head, covering the bare space between the beard ends. Attach two $^1/8$" peach balls for ears and use the round end of the pin to indent.

5 **Face:** Flatten two $^3/16$" pink balls and place $^1/8$" apart $^1/4$" above the beard. Press a $^1/8$" pink ball above the center of the beard for the mouth. Use the rounded end of the pin to indent. Shape two $^3/8$" white balls into flat teardrops. Attach for the mustache, curling the tips upward. Attach a $^1/4$" peach ball for the nose.

6 **Hat:** Roll a $1^1/4$" red ball into a $1^1/2$" long cone with a 1" base. Use your thumb to hollow the base. Attach to the top of the head. Fold the top of the hat down and forward as shown. Attach an $^11/16$" white ball to the top of the hat. Roll a $^5/8$" white ball into a 4" long log. Flatten to $^1/4$" wide. Start at the center back and wrap for the brim, resting the bottom edge on the ears and nose. **Holly:** Flatten two $^3/16$" green balls and shape to match the leaf pattern (see page 98). Indent the center of each with the pin and press together on the right side of the brim. Attach three $^1/16$" red balls to the center of the leaves.

7 **Reindeer—Legs:** Shape four $^11/16$" brown balls into $^3/4$" long tapered logs. Press the legs together. Flatten four $^3/8$" dark brown balls to $^7/16$" wide. Cut a slash in one side of each for the hooves. Attach one to the end of each foot, slashes forward. **Body:** Shape a $1^1/8$" brown ball into an egg. Press onto the top of the legs with the wide end at the back. Shape a $^7/8$" brown ball into an egg. Attach to the front of the body, narrow end up for the head. Shape a $^3/8$" brown ball into a cone and attach for a tail.

8 **Harness:** Roll a $^7/16$" green ball into a 5" long log, then press flat. Wrap it around the body. Cut off the excess and use it to wrap around the front connecting with the harness as shown. Cut off the excess.

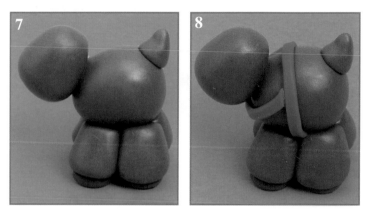

9 **Face:** Insert the seed beads (see page 7) for eyes. Attach a $^3/16$" red ball under the eyes for the nose. Use the pin to draw eyelashes and eyebrows. Indent a line under the nose. Shape two $^3/8$" brown balls into teardrops. Press onto the head for ears. **Bells:** Press four $^3/16$" yellow balls onto the harness across the back. Use the pin to mark an "X" on each.

10 **Antlers:** Shape two $^3/8$" tan balls into rounded triangles. Attach one to each side of the head, above the ears. Use the pin to indent into individual points. **Top Knot:** Roll a $^3/16$" brown ball into a $^1/2$" long log. Cut into two unequal lengths and attach side by side to the top of the head. **Holly:** Flatten two $^1/8$" green balls and shape to match the leaf pattern. Indent the center of each with the pin and press together as shown. Attach two $^1/16$" red balls to the center of the leaves. Bake (see page 6).

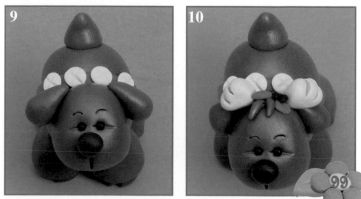

Hiking bear by Judy Ferrill

First, blend to make:
- medium brown: ¼ package of terra cotta + ¼ package of ivory
- gray: 1" white ball + ⅝" black ball

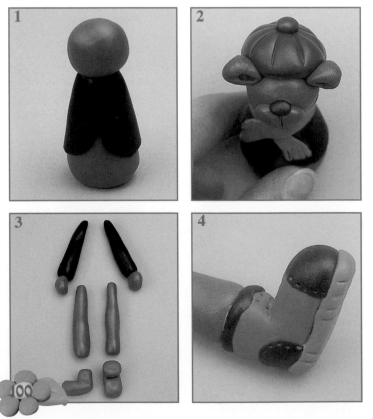

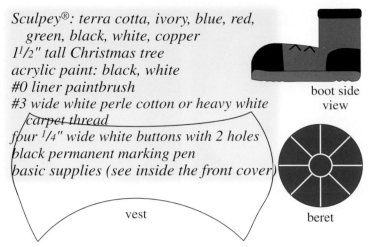

Sculpey®: terra cotta, ivory, blue, red, green, black, white, copper
1½" tall Christmas tree
acrylic paint: black, white
#0 liner paintbrush
#3 wide white perle cotton or heavy white carpet thread
four ¼" wide white buttons with 2 holes
black permanent marking pen
basic supplies (see inside the front cover)

boot side view

vest

beret

1 **Body:** Shape a 1⅛" medium brown ball into a 1⅝" tall cone. **Vest:** Flatten red to ¹/₁₆" thick. Lay the pattern on the clay and cut around it. Wrap around the body, barely overlapping the front edges. **Head:** Roll a ¾" ball of medium brown and attach (see page 7).

2 Flatten a ⁵/₁₆" medium brown ball into an oval and attach for his muzzle. Imprint a line down the muzzle center. Attach a ⅛" black ball for his nose. **Beret:** Flatten a ⅝" blue ball to ⅞" across and press onto his head. Use a toothpick to draw seam lines, dividing it into eight gores as shown on the pattern. Flatten a ³/₁₆" blue ball to ¼" across and attach to the hat center. **Ears:** Roll two ⁵/₁₆" medium brown balls, flatten each slightly and use the paintbrush handle to indent a hole. Attach one on each side of the beret. **Scarf:** Flatten green to ¹/₁₆" and cut a ¼"x3½" strip. Use the knife to fringe the ends, then wrap around his neck.

3 **Arms:** Roll two ⅜"x1½" red logs, thinning each to ¼" at the upper end. Roll two ⁷/₁₆" medium brown balls, flatten each slightly and attach to the bottoms of the arms for the paws. **Legs:** Make as for the arms, but use medium brown clay and omit the paws. **Boots:** Roll two ⅜"x1¼" green logs. Turn up ¼" on one end of each and attach the turned-up ends to the bottoms of the legs. Hold each leg upright and press the boot onto the work surface to flatten the bottom.

4 Roll a ⅛"x4" rope of copper; cut in half. Wrap one length around the seam at the top of each boot. Join and smooth the ends; flatten slightly. Flatten a ¼" copper ball to ¹/₁₆" thick. Drape over the toe of one boot, curving it to fit and wrapping the excess under. Repeat at the heel area of the boot, then for the other boot. Roll two ½" gray balls and flatten each into an oval to fit the bottom of a boot. Attach and draw tread lines with the toothpick. Imprint stitching lines around the toe and heel patches. Draw two X's on each boot for bootlaces. **Energy bar:** Flatten white to ⅛" thick and cut a ⅜"x¾" rectangle. Lay flat to bake. Pierce, bake, finish and assemble (see inside the back cover) the bear. Glue the tree into one hand as shown in the large photo. Use the pen to write "ENERGY BAR" on the bar; lacquer; let dry and glue into his other hand.

Reinhard Reindeer
by Judy Ferrill

Sculpey®: raw sienna, ivory, black
2 black seed beads
9" of ¹/₈" wide red satin ribbon
#3 wide white perle cotton or heavy white
carpet thread
four ¹/₄" wide white buttons with 2 holes
black permanent marking pen
small foam paintbrush
basic supplies (see inside the front cover)

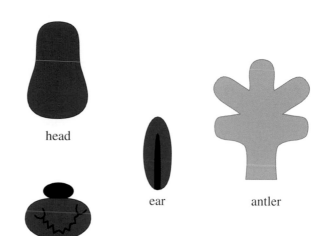

head

ear

antler

muzzle

1 **Body:** Shape a 1¹/₈" raw sienna ball into a 1¹/₂" tall cone. Shape a ³/₄" raw sienna ball into a 1" tall pear shape to match the head pattern and attach (see page 7) it to the body. Flatten a ³/₈" raw sienna ball into a ⁵/₈" wide oval and attach for his muzzle. Flatten a ¹/₄" black ball on top of the muzzle for his nose. Push in the seed beads for eyes.

2 **Ears:** Flatten two ³/₈" raw sienna balls into ⁵/₈" long ovals and shape each around the wooden end of a paintbrush as shown. Attach extending outward. **Antlers:** Flatten two ³/₄" ivory balls into ³/₁₆" thick ovals. Referring to the pattern, cut four V-shaped notches from the top of each; shape the bottom to a stem. Attach one behind each ear.

3 **Arms:** Roll two ³/₈"x1⁵/₈" raw sienna logs. Roll one end of each arm slightly thinner; use the side of a toothpick to imprint a cloven hoof division in the other end. **Legs:** Roll two ³/₈"x1³/₄" raw sienna logs. Imprint hoof divisions as for the arms.

4 Pierce, bake and assemble (see inside back cover). Use the black pen to draw eyebrows and a squiggly mouth. Seal the nose. Use the ribbon to tie a shoestring bow with ³/₈" loops and ¹/₂" tails; glue to his neck.

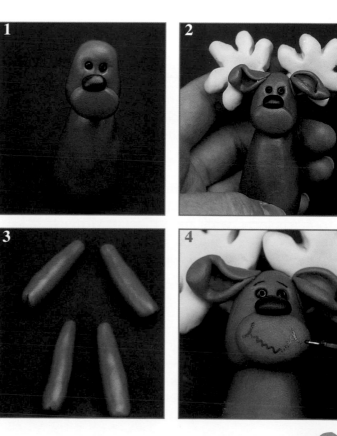

Gift-Bearing Santa
by Anita Behnen

Sculpey®: beige, raw sienna, red pearl, gold, ivory
red chalk, small paintbrush
white acrylic paint
wood bucket, hot coffee or tea
1" square of red/green/cream checked fabric
1" long sprig of green artificial pine
2 size 12/0 black seed beads
star clay cutters: 3/16", 5/16", or use these
1/2 tsp. of white embossing powder
stiff toothbrush
white snow-texture paint
fine iridescent clear glitter
basic supplies (see inside the front cover)

First, knead the embossing powder into a 1½" ball of red pearl to make speckled red. Stain the bucket by dipping it into hot coffee or tea; let dry.

1 Body: Shape a ⅞" black ball into a 1" tall egg. Break a toothpick into thirds. Insert ⅓ into the body top so ¼" extends. Insert two into the body bottom angled apart to support the boots. **Boots**: Shape two ¹¹/₁₆" balls of black clay into 1" long tapered logs. Bend each in half; pinch the bend to form the heel, then round the toe. Press the tapered ends onto the lower toothpicks.

2 Coat: Roll out speckled red to ¹/₁₆" thick and cut a 3" circle. Cut the circle in half. Set one half aside for step 9. Wrap the other around the body, draping it over the boots and overlapping the straight edge in the front (trim if necessary so the front is vertical).

3 Sleeves: Shape two ½" balls of speckled red into 1" long tapered logs. Bend each at the elbow. Insert the stylus into the wide end of each and rotate to form a hole ¼" wide and ¼" deep. **Mittens**: Shape two ⁷/₁₆" black balls into ¾" long tapered logs. Pinch to slightly flatten the wide ends. Insert the tapered ends into the sleeve holes so ⅜" extends.

4 Fur trim: Roll ivory to ⅛" thick. Texture with a stiff toothbrush. Cut into ¼" wide strips. Starting from the bottom front of the coat, press the trim along the bottom edge, then up the front. Join the ends smoothly and cut off excess. Use the toothbrush to re-texture where ends were blended. Cut a 1" length and press around each cuff. Save the rest for step 9.

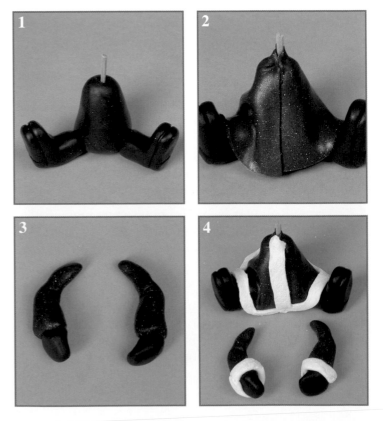

5 Glue the sleeve tops to the shoulders of the coat, with the wrists resting on the coat bottom. Glue the bucket back to the coat front. Glue the inside of the right mitten to the side of the bucket. Cut a slit into the left mitten and pinch it around the bucket handle. **Optional**: Bake (see page 6) for ten minutes. Let cool completely before handling.

6 **Head**: Shape a ⅝" beige ball into an egg. Insert the seed beads for eyes. Press the head onto the neck toothpick. Blush the cheeks.

7 **Beard**: Shape a 9/16" ivory ball into a 1" long teardrop. Turn the teardrop wide end up. Pinch to form corners and pull them out, shaping a scoop at the top. Attach to the face halfway as shown. Press the corners firmly onto the cheeks.

8 **Mustache**: Shape a ¼" ivory ball into a 1" long log with tapered ends. Attach over the beard so the tips curve downward. Use the pin to indent the center. **Nose**: Roll a ⅛" beige ball into an oval and press onto the mustache top. Blush the top of the nose. **Hair**: Shape five or six ¼" ivory balls into snakes of various lengths. Attach as shown.

9 **Hat**: Wrap the remaining half circle of speckled red around the hair and smooth the seam at the back. Press a strip of fur around the hat, joining the ends in the back. Use the toothbrush to retexture the joints if necessary. Twist the hat tip 2–3 times and bend to the right.

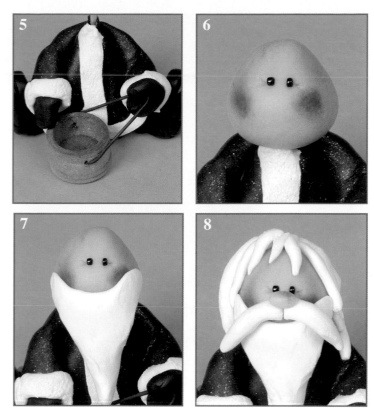

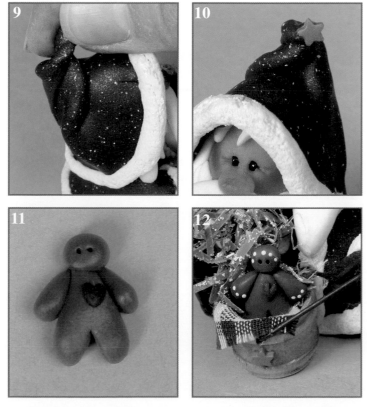

10 Flatten gold to 1/16" thick and use the cutters to cut two 3/16" and one 5/16" star. Attach a 3/16" star to the hat tip. Glue the other to the center of the bucket. Set the 5/16" star aside for step 12.

11 **Gingerbread boy**: Shape a 5/16" sienna ball into a ½" tall cone. Cut ¼" up from the wide end to form legs. Shape two 3/16" sienna balls into teardrops and attach for arms. Attach a 3/16" sienna ball for the head. Slightly flatten the cookie. Shape a ⅛" red ball into a teardrop and flatten. Cut ⅓ of the way down from the wide end to make a heart and press onto the left chest. Use the pin to indent the eyes.

12 Bake Santa, the 5/16" star and the cookie. Check during baking; if the white trim begins to brown, turn the oven temperature down 15°–20° to finish baking. Let cool. Dip a toothpick into white paint and make three dots on each cookie hand. Make five dots on the top of the face. Trim the pine sprig to look like an evergreen tree. Apply snow paint to the tree, Santa s boots and the hat trim. While it s still wet, sprinkle glitter on the tree. Let dry. Glue the 5/16" star to the tree top. Glue the fabric into the bucket. Glue the tree into the bucket back and the gingerbread boy into the front.

Santa's Helpers
by Shohreh Dolkhani

Sculpey®: tan, brown, red, green, black
5¹/₂"x2¹/₂"x1¹/₂" wood block
¹/₄" square stencil
six 1" long Y-shaped twigs
acrylic paints: red, light blue, black, white
paintbrushes: ¹/₂" flat, #0 liner
pink powder blush
stiff toothbrush
broad-tip black permanent pen
basic supplies (see inside the front cover)

actual width 5$\frac{1}{2}$"

1 **Dancer:** Shape four $\frac{1}{2}$" tan balls into $\frac{3}{4}$" long tapered logs. Press together. Push $\frac{1}{2}$" lengths of toothpick into the tops, leaving $\frac{1}{4}$" exposed. **Body:** Shape a $\frac{7}{8}$" tan ball into an egg. Press onto the top of the legs. Push a $\frac{1}{2}$" length of toothpick into the top front, leaving $\frac{1}{4}$" exposed. **Head:** Shape a $\frac{3}{4}$" tan ball into a rounded triangle. Press onto the body toothpick. Blush the cheeks.

2 **Ears:** Shape two $\frac{5}{16}$" tan balls into teardrops. Press one onto each side of the head. **Nose:** Shape a $\frac{3}{16}$" black ball into a rounded triangle. Press onto the face. Use the pin to draw a vertical line under the nose. **Tail:** Press a $\frac{3}{8}$" tan ball onto the rump.

3 **Bow:** Roll a $\frac{1}{16}$"x1$\frac{1}{2}$" red log. Wrap around the neck. Flatten red clay to $\frac{1}{16}$" thick and cut a $\frac{1}{4}$"x1$\frac{1}{4}$" strip. Flatten to $\frac{1}{16}$" thick. Fold the outside corners together and pinch the center. Press the bow onto the right side of the neck. **Antlers:** Push two twigs into the top of the head between the ears. **Prancer:** Repeat steps 1–3, placing the bow on the left instead of the right. **Rudolf:** Repeat steps 1–3, but use these balls: body—1" brown ball; head—$\frac{7}{8}$" brown ball; ears—$\frac{3}{8}$" brown balls; nose—$\frac{1}{4}$" red ball; bow—$\frac{1}{4}$"x1$\frac{3}{4}$" green strip. Make brown legs 1$\frac{1}{8}$" long. Bake (see page 6). Paint eyes (see page 7) on each reindeer.

4 **Base:** Paint the wood block red. Let dry. Stencil two rows of white checks on each end of one 5$\frac{1}{2}$"x1$\frac{1}{2}$" side. Spatter (see inside the back cover) white, then black paint on the front. Use the fine-tip pen to draw a —||— border around the front. Use the broad-tip pen to write "Santa's Helpers" inside the border. Make black dip dots on the ends of the letters. Glue the reindeer to the top of the base as shown. Cover the exposed block with moss.

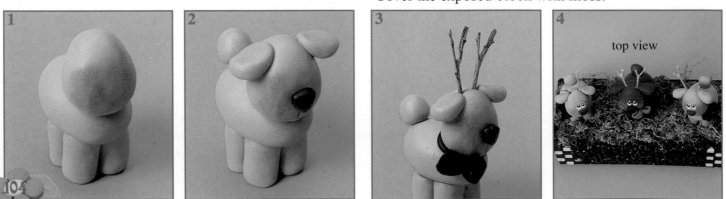

top view